BRIGHT IDEAS
FOR YOUR HOME

BRIGHT IDEAS
FOR YOUR HOME

THUNDER BAY
P·R·E·S·S

First published in the United States by:
Thunder Bay Press
5880 Oberlin Drive
Suite 400
San Diego
CA 92121-9653
1-800-284-3580

Library of Congress Cataloging in Publication Data available upon request.

ISBN 1-57145-086-6

Colour separation by P+W Graphics, Singapore
Printed in Singapore by Tien Wah Press

ACKNOWLEDGEMENTS

The publisher would like to thank the following photographers and organisations
for their permission to reproduce the photographs listed:

ROBERT HARDING SYNDICATION: pages 2, 4, 11, 13, 21, 24, 25, 27, 35, 39, 41, 43,
48, 50, 55, 61, 67, 98, 99, 104, 107, 108, 109, 110, 112, 113, 114, 129,
133, 135, 141, 145 & 159

CAMERA PRESS: pages 7, 19, 106, 111, 137, 139 & 151

INTERNATIONAL INTERIORS: pages 15, 17, 47, 52, 75, 87, 115 & 131

ELIZABETH WHITING AND ASSOCIATES: pages 32, 33, 45, 59, 81, 89, 105 & 145

ABODE: pages 5 & 143

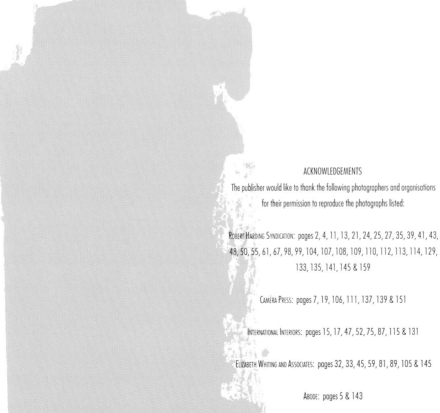

Contents

Introduction

If you want to create an original look for your home without spending a fortune, then here is your answer. This book provides the two vital ingredients for successful decorating – ideas and confidence. It includes a wealth of ideas for transforming all the most important rooms in your home with immense style but without spending correspondingly large amounts of money. Step-by-step directions give you the confidence and know-how to tackle the job and put these ideas into practice.

Whatever your dreams, you'll find your inspiration here. These pages are full of sound advice and practical tips for planning the perfect room – even on the smallest budget. You will learn how to transform dreary rooms with the minimum of effort – and materials – and also how to make the most of any disappointing features that you are stuck with. If you are lucky, you might be decorating from scratch, with the luxury of rooms that are the equivalent of a "blank canvas." However, most of us are not so lucky and have to work around the limitations imposed by existing colors, carpets or furnishings. In this book you will learn how to make these limitations work for you.

There are also 25 simple projects for you to enjoy. You don't have to be an expert to attempt these; enthusiasm is all that's required to achieve professional results – and save money at the same time.

Finally, this book shows you how to use tips from experienced interior designers, and assess your situation and needs very carefully before you start any work. Planning and prioritizing are essential if you are to achieve your aim of decorating in style on a tight budget.

From preparation to projects, you will find all that you need within these pages – practical, step-by-step projects combined with contemporary ideas and inspiration to help you transform your home.

Decorative screens provide a stylish yet thoroughly practical solution to the problem of multipurpose rooms.

Chapter one

Your bedroom

When you are planning a new look for your bedroom it can be tempting to dive straight in with the paintbrush or to buy a beautiful set of new furniture, but try to hold yourself back – for a while at least.

If you want to get really good results, you should go about the redesign of your bedroom in the way an interior designer would. Any professional will spend a lot of time discovering how you use the bedroom and what you want from it – before they even glance at their sample book. You should do the same: you want the bedroom to look great, but it must be practical, too. Everything in it has got to work for you or you will not enjoy spending time there – and after all, you spend at least a third of your life in bed.

This essential planning stage is referred to as "taking the brief" – in other words, gathering as much information as possible about the room and your needs. In order to do it properly, you will need to arm yourself with a notebook and tape measure. Then sit down in your bedroom, take a long hard look at it, and start to make notes. If you live with anyone else, it is worth asking them for their input at this stage (especially if it is their bedroom you are redesigning) so that there are no arguments later on.

You may not need to change everything about your bedroom. Perhaps you will keep the curtains and refresh the rest of the room scheme to complement them. It is often the fact that the carpet is worn and needs to be replaced that makes you want to give the room a facelift – would the rest of the scheme look better if you changed the carpet?

You need to think about all aspects of how the room looks and functions before you pick up a paintbrush – it's no good decorating and then deciding you need a new closet.

Opposite are some of the questions you should be asking yourself. If you are planning just a coat of fresh paint and moving the chest of drawers from one side of the room to another, this approach may seem excessive, but it really will help you to get the best out of your room. It may even save you from decorating again in just a few months' time.

Who does the room belong to?

This is crucial. You can design your own bedroom as a personal haven – somewhere to unwind and forget the stresses of the day surrounded by personal treasures. A guest bedroom requires a different approach. Although you will want it to reflect your own taste and ideas, it should also appear welcoming and comfortable to whoever comes to stay. A child's room demands yet another set of considerations, with practicality at the top of the list.

Is there any one thing in the bedroom – good or bad – that hits you when you walk through the door?

If so, you should concentrate on minimizing its impact. A good design is well balanced – that is, every element of the room should work in unison with the rest, rather than standing alone. Visitors should walk into your room and comment on how attractive the room is, not say, "Wow, what a lovely carpet."

Does the bedroom get much natural light?

If it doesn't, you will need to bear that in mind when it comes to choosing your color scheme. Most people want to create as much of an impression of light in a bedroom as possible, but if the room is small and dark, and you feel you are fighting a losing battle, you may consider emphasizing the room's more dramatic nature instead. You can afford to be more dramatic in your own bedroom than you would, say, in a guest bedroom, where you want everyone to feel at home.

Are there ways you might make the room lighter?

If your bedroom is in a corner of the house, could you add another window? Or, if you tend to keep your bedroom door closed, would you consider a door with a window? (The glass can be stained or frosted if you want to preserve your privacy.) These are decisions that should be made now – you don't want to start knocking down walls after laying a new carpet.

Which way does the bedroom face?

If you are a morning person, you will appreciate a bedroom that faces east, so you get the sun streaming in as you wake up. If you like sleeping late and the room faces the same way, you will want to invest in some well-lined curtains. The way a room faces also affects the type of light that a room receives. A north, east, or northeast-facing room will receive a colder light than those that face south, west, or southwest, and so will need a warmer color scheme (see Bedroom color, page 13).

How do you use your bedroom?

Obviously, by far the most important function of your bedroom is as a comfortable place to sleep, but it is likely that you do more than sleep there. You probably also use your bedroom as a place to store your clothes, get dressed, put on make-up, or read and watch TV, depending upon your lifestyle. If you have a lot of shelf and closet space, it may be that you use the room to store things from elsewhere in the house. Think about all the ways you use your bedroom and what would help to make that space

If space is short, make the most of every inch for useful storage areas – without sacrificing style.

9

more practical, as well as attractive. The following questions may point you in the right direction:

Could you benefit from having a sink installed?

If the mornings are always frantic in your house, an extra sink could reduce the pressure on the bathroom, giving you a place to wash, shave, or put on make-up in peace. If you have space, you could even put in a shower cubicle. A guest bedroom is also an ideal place to install a bathroom, and realtors claim that a connecting bathoom will make your house more saleable – if not more valuable.

Does anyone put on make-up in the bedroom?

If so, they will want a mirror that has both natural and artificial light. Remember that you are likely to use electrical equipment such as an electric razor and a hairdryer in front of the mirror, so you will need sockets nearby.

Are there enough mirrors in the room?

If the room is shared, it is worth having more than one mirror. The combination of a wall-mounted small mirror and a full-length mirror works well.

Do you watch television in bed?

It will need to be positioned appropriately, bearing in mind how light will reflect off the screen. Do you have an electrical socket in the right place or could it be installed easily?

Is the lighting adequate?

Bedside lights are essential, and you could adapt the wiring now so that one switch by your bed controls the various lights and lamps around the room. If you share the bedroom, does one person like to read while another goes to sleep? If so, you might consider a bedside lamp which can direct light on to a book without casting a glare around the room (see Bedroom lighting, page 19).

Do you have enough storage space?

If you rely heavily on underbed storage space, an elegant iron bedstead will be out of the question. Is there room to incorporate more expansive built-in storage, or is there an alcove you could use as a closet? (Turn to page 28 for how to turn a simple shelving unit into attractive storage.) Maybe you have an adjacent spare bedroom that could be adapted into a dressing room. If so, it will need hanging space, good lighting, and a full-length mirror.

Is the bedroom also a workspace?

Guest rooms are most likely to have a dual function and need to be carefully designed – especially their storage space, as you will need to pack away your things whenever anyone comes to stay. A table can act as both a desk and dresser and a chest of drawers can double as a filing cabinet.

What is your budget?

Before you go shopping, you need to set a top figure – then take off ten percent for unplanned expenditures. Once you know how much you can afford to spend, it is up to you to juggle the budget. If you have set your heart on a designer wallpaper, that's fine, but you may have to make do with cheaper curtains and bedlinen.

When you start to shop for the furniture and furnishings, keep a note of the price of everything; then before you part with any money, add it all up. It is the only way to keep within your means.

You may want to start a notebook for all your plans, perhaps with a folder for brochures and invoices. It will be useful for checking details in the future and an interesting reminder in years to come.

Making the most of existing furnishings

If you have already worked out your budget for your bedroom redesign, you will have an idea of what you can afford to replace and what you will have to live with for a while. However, if the prospect of living with the old carpet is just too much to bear, look at your priorities again – maybe you can cut a few corners elsewhere and replace the carpet after all. Look for end-of-season sales – you may find a remnant that fits the bedroom floor perfectly (especially if it is a small room).

Inevitably, however, there will be some inherited horrors that have to stay put – so here's how to make the most of them.

The old bed: When you dream wistfully of an elegant four-poster, being faced with a dingy daybed is a bit of a blow. However, there is no reason why you can't transform your existing bed into the one of your dreams – or something close to it at least. The features that give a bed its style and personality are the headboard and the bedlinen – so cast a critical look over the existing bed to see if there is anything you can do to transform these things.

If the headboard has seen better days, take it off. You could replace

Take another look at your existing furniture – it is so easy to rejuvenate wooden chests and dressers with a coat of paint. You could always stencil a design to match the room scheme.

Existing features

Even if this is your first home, it is unlikely that you will be in the enviable position of starting completely from scratch, able to buy everything you want brand new. Most of us have to accept that, for a while at least, we will have to live with an old bed, a thrift-shop chest, or an ancient carpet.

We also have to live with the existing structure of the house and any problems that may present. Unless you have an unlimited budget, knocking down walls, raising ceilings, and putting in new windows may be out of the question. Even if money were no object, structural alterations are not always advisable – a house soon loses its original character if it falls victim to every owner's whims.

Do not despair. With just a few clever decorating tricks and a little confidence, you can conceal a lot of the features you are unhappy with and make the most of others – without spending a fortune or calling in builders. In fact, some of the most challenging rooms turn out to be the most successful in the end.

it with a new one (if you can afford it) or scour a few architectural-salvage companies to see if you can get an antique cast-iron bedstead – they are often cheaper than the

reproductions. Another option is to make your own headboard out of composite board and either paint it or cover it in a pretty fabric. Turn to page 23 to find out how.

You don't need a four-poster to enjoy beautiful bed drapes. It is cheap and easy to hang simple drapes from a coronet above your bed. You could even cheat and simply staple or Velcro® light fabric drapes to a piece of board above the bed. If you still hanker after a real four-poster, take a look at bed frames instead. These can be made to fit around your existing bed and cost a fraction of the price of the real thing.

Now turn to the bedlinen. Covering your bed with an assortment of throw pillows is an instant way of giving your bed a facelift, but if more serious measures are needed, you could make or buy a new duvet or bedspread and some smart pillowcases. There is no need to spend a fortune. Plain sets of bedlinen are the cheapest on the market, but can look really special when trimmed with ties or buttons, decorated with fabric paints, or edged with a pretty ruffle (see page 26).

The dreadful carpet: If you are faced with a carpet that has seen better days, you may have to think twice before ripping it up. If the problem is simply a few bare patches, try rearranging your furniture to cover the worst of them, and investing in a rug or two to position strategically. If the carpet is simply not to your taste, you could buy a cheap rug to cover most of it and then site your furniture over the rest.

Check the state of the floor beneath the old carpet. If you are lucky, you may discover some perfect floorboards or parquet just waiting to be renovated. Bare boards look stylish as well as being hardwearing and cheap. You can either protect them with a coat of varnish or give them a stenciled or pickled finish (see page 31). Simply add a rug at the bedside to provide a comfortable landing spot when you get up in the morning.

Ugly furniture: Plain, shabby, and cheap pieces of furniture can be transformed into something quite special with just a little time and attention. Take another look at that old chest. Could the handles or feet be changed? How would it look if the paint or varnish were stripped off and restored? Perhaps it could be painted or stenciled to match your color scheme. (Turn to page 34 to find out how to color wash a bedside table.)

Deceiving the eye

You may not be able to change the actual structure of your bedroom, but you can certainly alter the impression the room gives by emphasizing certain aspects and concealing others. Here are some solutions to common problems:

Ceilings: Too little attention is given to ceilings. We spend weeks deliberating over the colors for walls, floors, and furniture, then simply slap a bit of white latex up above it all. Yet the height of your ceiling or, more accurately, the perceived height of your ceiling, can alter the whole feel of a room. By using color cleverly, you can make a startling difference to that perception.

Making it lower: A bedroom should make you feel relaxed and warm, but it probably won't if the ceiling appears cold and high. Make the ceiling appear to be lower by painting it a deeper or warmer shade than the walls. You could even use a patterned relief paper. Add a dado and extend the ceiling color down to it for extra effect, and perhaps decorate the walls in horizontal stripes to emphasize the width rather than the height.

Making it higher: In modern houses, the opposite problem is often the case. You may want to emphasize the quaint low ceilings by continuing the paint or wallpaper up and over them. Or you may want to make the ceiling recede and appear higher, in which case you could settle for white. Try using a pale pastel shade, lighter than the walls, to achieve the same effect. Vertical stripes will emphasize the height of the walls and appear to lift the ceiling.

Making it larger: You can make a room appear larger than it is by choosing light shades for the walls and furnishings.

The scale of furniture in the bedroom will also alter your perception of space. A four-poster bed is a bad choice if you want a room to look larger. Look for a lower bed and slim built-in closets that make the most of alcoves. Allow the eye to travel over the furniture and prevent any one piece from overpowering the room. Solid wall-to-wall carpets will create an impression of space.

Bedroom color

You can buy the most beautiful furniture and furnishings for your bedroom, but if you lack confidence and skill when it comes to color, the finished result will not be very effective.

Deciding on a scheme, choosing what colors go with which, and then putting together samples can be a daunting prospect. So how do you put together a successful color scheme for your bedroom?

Forget the particular color conundrums your bedroom is posing for a few minutes, and take a wider view. Some people are said to have a good eye for color – and maybe they have – but that does not mean that color skill can't be learned. In fact, just a little basic color theory will take you a long way. It may sound far removed from the immediate problem of choosing wallpapers, but if you understand how colors work in theory, it will make every decision a lot easier in practice.

Some of the most effective and striking color schemes use shades that you would not necessarily associate with bedrooms — lime green and shocking pink work wonderfully, and you can always use them as accents.

The color wheel

This is a basic way of demonstrating how combinations of certain colors produce other colors (red and blue produce purple, for example). The wheel becomes more useful to interior designers when you learn that it can be divided into halves – one half containing all the warm colors (red, red/orange, orange, yellow/orange, and yellow, and their various tints and shades) and the other the cool colors (green, blue/green, blue, and blue/violet, and their tints and shades). The warm colors are also known as advancing colors, as they have the effect of appearing to be closer to you than the cooler colors on the other side of the wheel, which appear to recede.

Putting theory into practice

You can use the warm side of the color wheel to warm a bedroom, and the cool colors to make it appear bigger and airier. Remember though that the darker shades of any color, including green and blue, will make your bedroom appear smaller than a pastel shade. Try not to let the size of your bedroom deter you from considering the darker shades completely. Even a small bedroom can look dramatic in deep blue.

Think about the effect you want to achieve. The person using the room should be your first consideration. For a child's bedroom, bright primary colors are lively, fun, and more stimulating than the traditional pastel pinks and blues. For a guest room, a universally appealing color such as blue would work well in a room that faces south or west and so gets a warm light – especially when teamed with warm yellow.

In your own bedroom, you are free to indulge your fancies. For traditional impact go for deep-red walls – but nothing too bright or it will be so stimulating you won't be able to sleep.

Different colors have been proven to produce certain psychological effects. Blue is the color of harmony and peace, perfect for a tranquil bedroom. Yellow is a more joyful color associated with creative energy and power. Rich violet and mauve are reminiscent of church pageantry and inspire meditative thought. Pink is suggestive of passion and caring.

Although some color schemes use just one color and then accessorize it with tints and shades of the same hue, most schemes incorporate an accent color picked from the opposite side of the color wheel. If you fancy a romantic pink bedroom, add touches of cool blue or green to balance the warmth. By restricting accent colors to bedlinen and perhaps lampshades, it is cheap and easy to change the mood of your bedroom from time to time.

Incorporating existing furnishings

It can actually help to have existing furnishings that need to be incorporated into the scheme. If it is your old carpet that can't be replaced and it is a color you are not fond of, take your main color from the opposite side of the color wheel and use the carpet just as an accent. If you decide to use it as the major color in the room, then look for paint or wallpaper in a similar shade and select an accent color from the opposite side of the color wheel.

If your existing carpet, curtains, or bedspread incorporate several different colors, you are lucky – your color scheming has been done for you. Pick one hue as your main color to use on the walls and use the others as accents.

Staying neutral

Neutral shades such as cream, gray, and especially white are extremely versatile and can be used as an extra accent color in almost any color scheme. (Black is also regarded as a neutral color, but it can be harsh and should be used sparingly.) You could create a bedroom scheme from neutral shades alone. The trick is to extend the range of shades beyond white to cream, ocher, coffee, and maybe degrees of gray. Then use pattern and texture for extra interest.

Making color work

Color and pattern can be used to emphasize features and areas within the room. Alcoves, window frames, or the wall behind your bed can be treated in a deeper or contrasting shade, and areas with dedicated functions such as washing or studying can also be defined with different colors.

Positioning your furniture

The way you place your furniture can alter the whole effect of the room, making it appear spacious or cluttered, quirky or traditional. Be as imaginative as you can, although it has to be said that an average-sized bedroom offers little flexibility – basically because the pieces you need to juggle are so large. Experiment with a screen, a blanket box and maybe a circular table to create little areas of interest within the room, and avoid putting every piece of furniture slap up against the wall.

Practical positioning

It is usual to avoid putting the head of a bed directly under a window or up against a radiator (to avoid both drafts and over-heating and, in a children's room, to prevent accidents from happening if they jump on the bed). This may eliminate two of your four walls immediately, and if one of the other two has either a fireplace or an awkwardly placed door, you are likely to be left with just one place for your bed.

You may find you have very little choice about where to position the bed. If so, experiment with the smaller pieces of furniture in different places around the bed until you find an arrangement you are happy with.

Bedroom furniture

Abedroom may not need much in the way of furniture, but the basic pieces it does require – bed, chest, and perhaps a dresser – all need to work hard for you. To get the perfect balance of style and practicality within your budget, you'll need to do some thorough planning and research. Before going shopping, take a good look at what you have already and ascertain whether you do actually need anything else. Make sketches of each wall in your bedroom to decide how you want the room to look, where your existing furniture could go, and what else you may need to buy.

Remember to leave space for bedside tables. If you want bedside lamps, you'll need conveniently positioned electrical sockets, too. Now is the time to call an electrician if you think you will need extra sockets. But make sure you have definitely decided where the bed will go first.

Check that there is room to open a closet door easily, sit comfortably at a dresser and move around in front of a mirror.

Planning on paper

Bedroom furniture is big and heavy, so to avoid straining your back shifting it around the room, do your experimenting with a plan on paper first.

Transfer your floor measurements onto graph paper using a scale that allows you to fit your entire plan on to a sheet – 1:20 is normally adequate. Mark on it your sockets, windows, radiators, TV plug and the direction the door opens. Now measure the width and depth of the furniture which is staying in the room. Adapt the measurements to the same scale and cut them out of graph paper. Label each piece and move them around until you get an arrangement that works. Then trace your plan, complete with positioned furniture, onto tracing paper and put it to one side.
You may find you have to do several such tracings with the furniture in different positions until you find an arrangement you like, but you can compare them more easily if they are all in front of you at once.

Choosing a bed

Embarrassing though it may be, the only way to decide what sort of bed will suit you is to actually lie on it in the store. Take your time. Buying a bed is an expensive business, and you want to be sure to make a good choice. Experiment with different bases and mattresses until you find a combination that feels right.

Mattresses

There are two basic types of mattress – those with a spring interior and those made of only foam, fiber or latex. You will probably be considering spring mattresses, and these are also divided into two types – pocket spring and open spring. Pocket springs are housed in little fabric pockets that move independently so that your body gets support where it needs it. They are generally more expensive than open-spring mattresses, which vary tremendously according to the number of springs used and the gauge of the wire.

Closets

For maximum storage space, the sensible option is to have a built-in closet. This space can be designed to your own specifications and will provide room for suitcases, hat boxes and evening dresses – great for minimizing clutter around your bedroom. The most sophisticated designs can hold dressers and televisions – all cunningly and neatly concealed behind a streamlined finish. Large closets can hold chests of drawers inside, which frees up floor space in the bedroom itself and reduces clutter.
At the very least you will need hanging space for jackets and for full-length clothes such as coats and dresses. You may also find it useful to have special racks for storing shoes.
If the room doesn't have a closet, you can possibly have one built into an alcove or along one wall of the room if it is big enough to sacrifice the floor space. Otherwise, consider an old-fashioned armoire and a chest of drawers or two. Armoires can be attractive pieces of furniture, but they tend to be quite small when compared to a closet, so they may well not give you adequate space for your needs.

Chests

Chests of drawers range from tiny to huge, and from traditional to sleekly ultramodern. They can be located readily in secondhand stores or bought as flat-packs for self-assembly from department stores and furniture outlets. Most are straightforward to put together and can be decorated in a choice of finishes to match your color scheme.

Points to consider

There is a multitude of different window dressings to choose from – which makes decision-making difficult. However, if you focus on your own particular needs, it will make the process easier.

First of all consider the following points: your window type and what it overlooks, the style or theme of your bedroom, and the amount of light the bedroom receives.

The size and design of your windows will rule out certain styles immediately. Swags and tails are rather grand for most bedrooms and will look incongruous against modern picture windows, while slatted blinds do little for tiny window casements. Full-length curtains usually need a tall window in order to look balanced, and more imposing designs require an equally grand frame.

If you use your bedroom purely as a place to sleep, the amount of natural light that the bedroom receives will be less of an issue than the artificial lighting you choose. However, you may want to get as much light as possible in order to put on make-up or study – or simply because it makes you feel happier. If your windows are small, full curtains and valances will make the bedroom too dark.

The simple tie-top curtains in this bedroom offer privacy while also allowing the sunlight to filter through. Add a blackout shade if you like to sleep in total darkness.

Curtains, blinds and drapes in the bedroom

Window dressings set the seal on the look of your bedroom, inside and out, so style and practicality are both important considerations. If you like to wake up with the sun streaming into your bedroom, heavy and elaborate curtains are the last thing you need – unless you are happy to leave them open at all times and simply pull down a sheer shade for a bit of privacy at night. However, if you are someone who likes to sleep until noon, you won't greet the morning sun with the same enthusiasm. Instead, the blackout qualities of whatever you choose will be crucial.

Instead, go for simple designs without low pelmets, and use tiebacks to open up the window area. Or you could extend your pole or track beyond the window frame so the curtains do not obscure the glass at all.

If your bedroom overlooks the street, or other houses look in, choose window dressings that offer a degree of optional privacy during the daytime, too. A combination of dressings, such as a flat light-filtering shade with curtains, works well, and on sunny days a blind will protect your furnishings, too.

Choosing a style

Curtains: These offer privacy, will help to keep you warm at night (especially if they are given a thermal lining) and with a blackout lining will keep the room dark during the day. Curtains finish and soften a bedroom window frame, but because of the amount of fabric it takes to make them look the part, they can add up to be a rather expensive option.

There is a vast selection of headings and styles available, from tab heads for a simple Shaker look and the more conventional pencil pleats, right through to swags, tails, rosettes, and shaped valances for a traditional feel. Choose the finish to suit your style, or if that is beyond your means, consider one of the budget options, below.

Blinds: Cheaper than curtains, blinds will also minimize drafts and offer privacy while allowing more control over the amount of light you let into your bedroom during the day. Roman, paper, and cane blinds and roll-up shades will roll or fold down to protect your room from the sun and other people's eyes, while slatted blinds can be adjusted to allow more or less daylight to filter through the slats.

All of these styles offer a minimalist effect which alone may be too severe for a bedroom, but they can be dressed up with one of the other finishes outlined below. Festoon and balloon blinds are more luxurious, with ruched fabric and ruffled edges, and are ideal for more feminine bedrooms.

Lace panels: These are a pretty way of allowing light to filter through the bedroom window while simultaneously offering privacy. They are available ready-made in a variety of lengths and make an attractive alternative to glass curtains. Combine them with curtains or a blind for extra privacy and warmth.

Shaped valances: Enjoying a revival, wooden valances are now being used in more exciting shapes which can be covered in fabric or painted to match your scheme. Combined with simple curtains, a valance can look very effective, but it also works well on a small window as a dressing on its own.

Dress curtains: If you want curtains only to create a frame for a blind and are never likely to close them across the window, you needn't waste money on lots of fabric: just buy one width or enough to frame the sides of your window adequately. If the curtains are light, you may even be able to dispense with conventional headings, too, by using touch-and-close tape instead. One length of the tape is sewn to your curtain and the other is stuck to the window surround, so you can simply "stick" your curtains up. You can also take them down easily for cleaning.

Cheap and easy

You don't need to spend a fortune on curtain fabric or even to be able to sew to dress your windows with flair. Just try some of these simple ideas for maximum effect from minimum effort:

Curtain clips: Instant curtains with no sewing required. These rings are just like normal curtain rings, but have a little clip at the bottom to hold up pieces of fabric, gauze or lace. Ideal for simply styled bedrooms or as a quick, temporary measure.

Swag holders: These make it easy to produce cheap and informal swagged valances – just feed fabric through two of these metal brackets mounted at the top of your frame. The holders create formal rosettes or allow the fabric to fall naturally. Use them alone over a blind or with curtains in a contrasting fabric. They are also good for draping fabric over your bed, with one holder placed high above the bed and two at bed height on either side.

Before you start

Your lighting system should be planned long before you lift a paintbrush since putting in extra sockets or additional wall lights inevitably means working on electrical wiring behind the wall and tends to make a bit of mess.

Take another look at your "brief" to remind yourself of what your lighting needs to achieve. A bedroom may require subtle romantic lighting, so think about how you can create it – and how you can adapt the wiring so that all lights can be turned off at the flick of just one switch.

Think about the overall effect that you want to create once the decoration is completed and the new furnishings are in place. Bright, bold color schemes will look their best with modern lighting. Traditional or pretty bedrooms need something a little more conventional.

Children might like a night light, so make sure that there are sockets by their beds for that, in addition to a bedside lamp and maybe a baby monitor, too.

Do you like to read while someone sleeps beside you? If so, you may want to install bedside lights which can be directed onto a page and will not disturb the other person in the room. Or do you have two children sharing a room? If so, they will each need a bedside light, particularly if they have different bedtimes. If the children sleep in bunk beds, their bedside lights could be mounted on the wall at

Bedroom lighting

Never underestimate the power of artificial light. At the flick of a switch, it can alter the mood and efficiency of your bedroom, transforming it instantly into a more welcoming place, spotlighting areas of interest and providing perfect illumination for reading, sleeping, putting on make-up, and mixing and matching clothes. You can spend ages choosing fabrics, wallpaper, and accessories, but if your lighting is ineffective, your bedroom will appear uninteresting and dull after dark – which is, after all, when you are most often there. Here's how to achieve good lighting in your bedroom.

You do not need table lamps to provide bedside lighting. Stylish pendants hanging from a long cord look chic – and can be controlled by a dimmer switch for extra flexibility.

the correct height for each bunk. The switches would need to be within reach of both bunks.

If you have a desk in the bedroom, you will need to think about the right sort of lighting for that. An adjustable angle light is usually the best option.

If you have already planned the position of your bedroom furniture on your scaled-paper plan, consider whether you have enough sockets for additional lamps in appropriate places. Check that there are sockets by your bedside tables, near the television, and handy for the mirror where you intend to shave or use a hairdryer. If there aren't, mark on your plan that you need extra sockets at those points.

If you are happy with the existing lighting in your bedroom, it may just be a matter of buying a few new lampshades to match the new decor or update the look.

Don't restrict yourself to table lamps when you are planning your lighting. There is a wide choice of fixtures available, each offering a unique style and direction of light. Knowing a little about all these different types will help you make the right choice.

Types of lighting

Ceiling lights: The most common light fixture of all, this is usually a pendant and shade in the center of the room. However, there are many other types of ceiling lights to choose from.
A pendant and shade direct the light mainly downward and

outward, according to the angle of the shade (although a lot of light is also lost through the hole in the top of the shade, sending light up to the ceiling); spotlights allow you to direct light wherever it is needed; recessed downlighters shine a beam of light directly downwards; domed ceiling fixtures give a diffuse light around the whole room.

Wall lights: One of the earliest forms of electrical fixtures, these are a more subtle source of light than central ceiling fixtures and ideal for bedsides where there is no room for a table and lamp.

The more modern wall lights are often uplighters, sending light up across the wall and onto the ceiling. They are useful for adding attractive pools of light, but are not so practical for reading or studying. Picture lights also fit into this category and can be set either above or below the painting or object you wish to illuminate.

Table lamps: These are useful for offering general lighting without resorting to the flattening glare of a central ceiling light. They also allow you to control more accurately which areas of the bedroom are lit.

Position table lamps around the room to create warm pools of light by the bed, on a dressing table and on top of chests of drawers or occasional tables. If possible, arrange your wiring so that you can turn on all table lamps at the flick of just one central switch as you walk into the room. You may need another switch by the bed.

Floor lights: These are less commonly found in the bedroom unless there is an armchair used for reading – in which case, a standard shade or a spotlight stand is more suitable than an uplighter.

Dimmer switches: Counteract the glare of an overhead light by replacing a standard switch with a dimmer. Cheap and easy to install, this will give you greater control over the lighting and is perfect for waking you slowly on a dark morning, casting a gentle light over children at night, or creating a soft light to soothe tired eyes at bedtime.

Candlelight: Candles are a soft and flexible light source, either freestanding on a mantelpiece, wall-mounted on a sconce, or hung centrally in a chandelier or lantern. Casting a flattering glow around the room, they create an ambience electric light will never match. Wherever you are in the house, candles should be treated with great caution. Never leave a candle burning unattended and do not light a candle at all if you are tired and there is a danger that you will fall asleep. Make sure the candlesticks are on a flat surface where they will not topple over, and as an extra safety precaution, whether you intend to use candles or not, you should install a smoke alarm in the bedroom.

Bedroom flooring

A bedroom is the one place where you can afford to be a bit more indulgent with your flooring. Of all the rooms in the house, it has to face up to the least traffic. Unless it is a child's room or you are particularly heavy-footed or clumsy, the worst it will have to deal with is some barefooted padding about in the morning and evening – and perhaps the occasional spill of coffee.

Hard or soft?

If you are not particularly bothered about putting your foot down onto something soft in the morning and are still undecided about the various merits of carpet and hard flooring, consider the following:

Hard flooring such as tile, parquet, or wood-strip will be tough as well as attractive. Wooden flooring is ideal for traditional-style bedrooms, ranging from country or Shaker through to a simple Victorian look. Tiles are a more unusual (and costly) option, but can look elegant or rustic depending on your choice of finish.

Continuing the checkered theme on to the flooring, this painted floor is cheap and easy to achieve.

Remember though that a bottle of perfume or aftershave will shatter if it hits a ceramic floor and your toes may get quite chilly in the winter.

All types of hard flooring will take spills in their stride and act as a usefully neutral setting to furniture and furnishings for years, however many times you decide to change your color scheme. Don't forget that to lay hard flooring, particularly tiles, you need a flat, solid floor, and it is best to call in a professional unless you are experienced at laying tiles.

Children's rooms

Hard flooring is especially useful in children's rooms since most types can be easily wiped down and cope well with even a bit of youthful artwork imposed on them. You will probably feel the need for a rug or two to soften the look, however, and that combined with the cost of the flooring (plus padding to prevent rugs from slipping) can work out to be rather expensive.

Wall-to-wall carpets

Carpeting, on the other hand, offers softness and warmth underfoot and a sense of wall-to-wall comfort. Its insulating qualities prevent every footstep from echoing around the house, and there is sure to be a version that suits your color scheme and bank balance. If you like to decorate and change your color schemes fairly frequently, it is more sensible to choose inexpensive carpet and replace it to match the other colors in the

room. However, if you choose a plain carpet in a neutral color you will be able to introduce new furnishings with no fear of clashing shades.

Don't forget to budget for the padding when you are doing your sums. Padding prolongs the life of a carpet, makes it softer to walk on, and improves its insulating qualities. Foam-backed carpets are cheaper but usually of inferior quality, and their life span is accordingly much shorter.

If you are considering carpet for a child's room, take a look at carpet tiles. These are made of heavy-duty materials and are easy to install and replace if there are accidents and spills, but they are available in only a limited choice of colors.

Choosing carpet for your room allows you to play with your newly acquired color theory and create illusions of space and warmth in your bedroom if necessary. Reds, oranges, yellows, and browns will have a warming effect, while blues and greens will cool the room.

Plain light-colored carpet laid wall-to-wall will make a room appear larger, whereas heavily patterned carpet in darker colors will have the opposite effect, though to a lesser extent. Plain carpet in either light or dark colors will show every stain and piece of fluff; patterns will allow you to get away with more. Take carpet samples home to get an impression of how they will look.

If you are still undecided, consider a third option – natural matting.

This is made from vegetable fibers such as sisal, coir, jute, and seagrass, and is tough and hardwearing while also offering some of the qualities of carpet – especially those varieties which combine the natural fibers with the softness of wool. Although colored natural flooring is becoming more widely available, it is most popular in natural shades which will complement any color scheme and suit most styles of bedroom except for the very lavish.

Wooden floors

If saving money is a priority, check what's underneath your existing carpet. You may be lucky enough to discover forgotten parquet or some decent floorboards which, with a little sanding and a few coats of paint and/or varnish, could be restored to a beautiful finish. (Turn to page 31 for details of how to give floorboards a pickled and stenciled finish.) Always check the entire floor before you start sanding; sometimes a small area is beyond repair or covered in concrete. If this is the case, you may need to replace the damaged floorboards, or even think again. If you really want a wood finish, you could opt for a combined veneer and laminate which will give a stylish tongue-and-groove look or a "parquet" finish, depending on whether you choose strips or tiles.

You will need
- Medium density fiberboard or plywood to fit your own specifications
- A sheet of paper as big as the board
- Jigsaw
- Foam rubber, 1-2 inches thick
- Pencil
- Scissors
- Tape measure
- Glue
- Material for board
- Piping
- Matching thread

Project 1

Making a headboard

If you don't like your existing headboard — ditch it! Why not, when it's so easy to make this chic fabric-covered alternative?

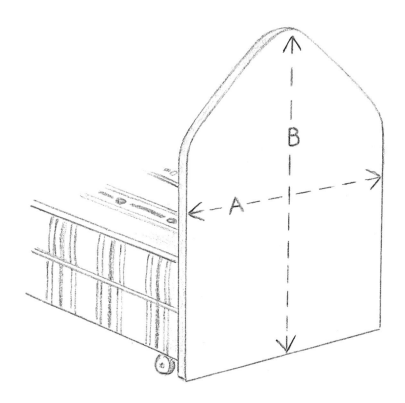

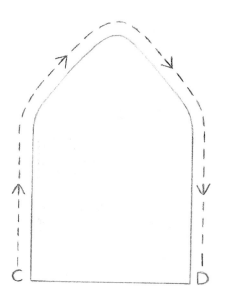

To make the board

1 Measure for your headboard by taking the width of your bed (A) and the height from the floor to the top of the base of the bed, plus 36 inches (B).

2 Make a paper pattern of the shape of the headboard to fit your measurements. It's easier if you fold the paper in half widthwise and draw half of the shape so that when you cut the pattern it is symmetrical. Open out the cut pattern and pin it to your board, then draw around it with a pencil or chalk. Keep the paper pattern for step 3 and cut out the shape carefully with a jigsaw.

3 Cut the foam to the same shape as the board, using the paper template again as a guide. Then cover the headboard with the foam — using glue to attach it — for added softness and depth.

To make the cover

The cover is made as a slip-on cover, similar to a pillowcase, with an opening along the lower edges.

1 Estimate the amount of fabric you need by measuring the sides and top edges of the board, plus 2 inches for working (C to D in the diagram on the preceding page). This will also be the measurement for the strip of material that links the two panels. The amount of piping needed will be double this measurement.

2 Cut out two pieces of fabric the size of the headboard plus ½ inch all round for seams. Cut a strip of fabric to fit around the sides and the top edges of the headboard, plus 1 inch for seams. Make this strip as deep as the padded headboard plus 1 inch for seams.

3 Take one of the fabric panels. With the right side facing you, place the piping on top, with the piping facing inward. On top of the piping, place the gusset strip that has been cut to fit around the sides. With the wrong side of the fabric facing you, pin together and then stitch

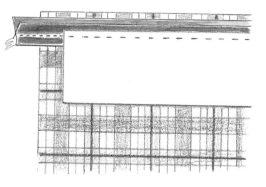

Variation

Tacky wooden headboards can be brought up to date with a coat of paint. Use eggshell or gloss paint for a hardwearing finish, and sand and prime the wood before you start. If you fancy a complex design, mark it with pencil before you start and let the paint dry thoroughly between coats.

around the sides ½ inch from the edge to form a flat seam.

4 Trim the corners and the seam allowances to about ¼ inch from the stitching.

5 Join the gusset strip and piping to the back section of the cover in the same way and finish.

6 Hem the open edge at the bottom by turning up ½ inch, then turning it again to make a double ¼ inch hem.

7 Press the cover and slip it over the headboard.

Project 2

Decorating plain pillowcases

Plain pillowcases can be given a new look by simply edging or decorating them. Take your inspiration from the design of your bedroom — for a romantic look, choose pretty eyelet lace, or for something more celestial try your hand at fabric stamping. If you are really adventurous, you could experiment with fabric paint and create a design of your own or one adapted from a pattern from your quilt, your curtains, or even a picture on the wall.

You will need

- Generously sized pillowcases
- A length of eyelet lace (depending on the size of your pillowcase and the type of trimming you choose)
- Thread to match
- Scissors

Eyelet lace trimming

1 Measure all four edges of your pillowcase. If you are planning to trim it with eyelet lace that has already been gathered, you will need to buy this amount, plus a little bit extra for working. If the trim you use has not yet been gathered, buy a length of lace one and a half times the measurement of the pillowcase to allow for the gathering.

2 If you have bought ungathered lace, or a similar edging material, stitch along the raw edge with a loose running stitch and gently gather it along the thread to create a ruffle.

3 Turn your pillowcase inside out and cut off the existing seams as close to the seam as you can, so that you lose as little space in the pillowcase as possible. Cut open the folded edges of the pillowcase too so that every edge is open.

4 Place your gathered trim between the front and back sections of the pillowcase with the lace turned inward to face the center of the pillowcase. Stitch the side seams together again, over the edge of the lace to attach it.

Finally, use a zigzag stitch over the raw edges to finish them.

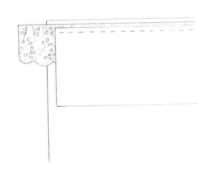

5 Turn the pillowcase right side out and press it.

To stamp a pillowcase

You can buy ready-made stamps and stamp paint from craft and fabric stores, or you could make your own from a potato. Cover the

base of the stamp evenly in paint, using a roller or a sponge, and practice on a similar piece of material, such as a handkerchief, before tackling the pillowcase.

Always recoat the stamp with fresh paint before you make each print, and work in such a way that you avoid smudging the prints you have recently done.

Variation

Give your duvet a unique finishing touch by adding fabric ties to the opening — they need not replace the existing fastening, simply enhance it. Turn to page 38 for instructions on how to make the fabric ties for the fabric-covered shelves and make your ties roughly 5 inches long. Once you have made enough pairs, pin them to the edge of your duvet cover at measured intervals to make sure you have enough and are happy with the look. If your duvet cover is fastened with buttons, position the ties as close to each button or snap as possible. Turn the duvet cover inside out and stitch each tie close to the edge, making sure that its partner is directly opposite it.

Project 3

Chic concealed storage

Why display clutter when you can conceal it behind this stylish fabric cover? Choose a fabric to complement your bedroom and use it to hide anything from sweaters to boxes.

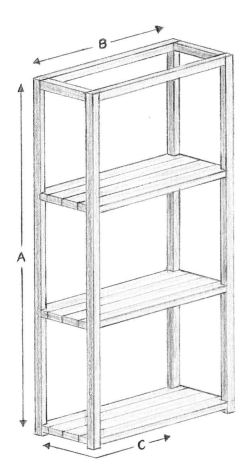

2 Cut out the side and back panels. For the back panel: mark the size of the panel (A by B, plus about ¾ inch all around for seams) on the fabric and cut it out. For the two side panels: mark the dimensions (A by C, plus about ¾ inch all around) on the fabric and cut it out.

3 Machine-stitch the three panels together (right sides of the fabric together) to form one large piece of fabric and hem the raw edges.

4 Measure the width and depth of the top of the shelving and mark this panel on your fabric. Now mark a line around the panel, ¾ inch wider all the way around. Cut the fabric around the outer line, then fold the fabric under along the inner line and press the crease.

Attach the top panel to the rest of the cover using a basting stitch with the right sides of the fabric together. Place the cover over the frame to check the fit; hand-stitch the panel on and remove the basting stitches.

1 Measure the shelving, taking the height (measurement A), the width (measurement B,) and then the depth plus half of the width (B) for measurement C.

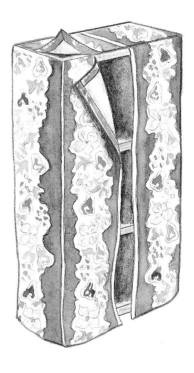

5 Finish the cover with a scalloped edge. Alternatively, you could equally point the ends, like pennants, or square them off. To make scallops, use a plate as a guide and trace the design onto paper. Check that the paper pattern fits across the top of the unit.

Measure around the top of the frame and cut a piece of fabric to that length, plus ¾ inch seam allowance, and 18 inches wide. Fold the fabric in half, lengthwise, with right sides together.

When you are happy with your paper scallops, use the paper pattern to mark the design along the length of the fabric.

6 Machine-stitch along the edges of the scallops, then cut out the shapes, a little less than ½ inch beyond your stitching. Clip the seam twice on each scallop to allow it to lie flat without rippling, then turn the scallops right side out and press them. Hand-stitch them to the edge of the roof panel.

7 Make two or three sets of fabric ties by cutting four strips of fabric, roughly 4 x 16 inches for two sets of ties. Fold each strip in half lengthwise, with right sides together, and stitch the raw edges together. Trim off any excess fabric, turn ties the right side out and press. Turn the raw ends inside and handstitch them down. Stitch the ties to the front of the cover.

Project 4

Pickling a bedroom floor

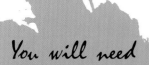

You will need

- White gloss paint (ideally the sort that only needs one coat)
- Mineral spirits
- A paint can
- A wide paint-brush
- A sponge
- Clear non-yellowing heavy-duty varnish (yacht varnish is ideal)

You don't have to splash out on real pickled wood to achieve the same cool and elegant look. By following these easy steps, you can achieve a pickled effect with just a can of white paint and a little mineral spirits.

1 Prepare the floor boards by vacuuming and cleaning them, then prime them with varnish thinned with mineral spirits — you will need to apply two coats, letting the boards dry thoroughly between coats.

2 Mix the gloss paint with an equal amount of mineral spirits in a paint can, then paint it on the boards with a brush, covering a small area at a time.

3 Before the paint dries, quickly wipe it with a dry sponge to give an uneven and soft pickled effect.

4 Protect the floor by sealing it with a couple of coats of heavy-duty varnish.

Variation

To give your floor a more decorative finish, you could stencil the edges of the room, and even decorate the middle, too. Choose a stencil with quite a large design, especially if the room is spacious; otherwise, it will look lost. Practice stenciling on paper first and position the paper stencil design on the floor to make sure you are happy with the look.

When you start to stencil, use a stencil brush and stencil paint, and keep your brush dry so that the finished look is subtle and almost faded. Use masking tape or spray mount to keep the stencil in place as you work and keep checking it for a build-up of paint so that it does not smudge.

Project 5
Color washing

Color-washed wood has a soft "aged" look which is perfect for the simple bedroom and easy to achieve. Before you treat any piece of wood in this way, you need to remove all existing paint or varnish with an appropriate stripper, and then sand it.

You will need
- A wire brush
- Latex paint
- Water
- A wide paint-brush
- A soft lint-free cloth or dry sponge
- Sandpaper
- Clear paste wax

1 After the wood has been prepared, open up the grain by rubbing the piece of furniture with a wire brush. This helps the wood grain to absorb the paint. Always work in the direction of the grain to avoid marking the wood.

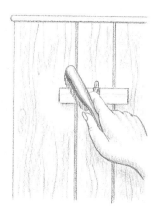

Variation
You can achieve a look similar to this chest using pickling wax or paste instead. Apply the paste with steel wool in a circular motion; then buff it with clear paste wax on a lint-free cloth.

2 Mix the paint with water using about six parts paint, one part water, and test the effect on a small area. Wash the paint roughly over the surface in the direction of the grain, treating just a small area at a time.

3 When the paint is nearly dry, wipe off the excess with a dry sponge or lint-free cloth until you can see the grain of the wood. Next day, sand the surface once more to finish and seal it with a clear paste wax.

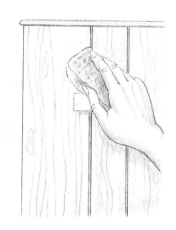

Chapter two

Your bathroom

The essence of all good design is thoughtful planning and research. So before you make any alterations to your bathroom, it is important to consider what already exists and how it might saved or changed as part of the new look. Once bathroom appliances are in place, it can be a costly business to start moving it around. Careful thought at the start of the job can save a great deal of money later.

Take a long hard look at the room; take note of its shape, height, size, and fixtures. Invest in a notebook, a folder for the many catalogs you are sure to gather, and some graph paper to draw a diagram of your bathroom to scale: then cut out pieces to the shape and size of fixtures and move them around on the paper until they describe your ideal layout.

What space do you have to work with?

The first question should be whether the bathroom is in the right place. Is it in a very large room that would be better used as a bedroom? Alternatively, if your bathroom is very small, do you have a spare room that could be converted into a larger bathroom? Can you remove a wall between the bathroom and an adjoining room to make more space? How about moving a partition wall and taking space from a neighboring bedroom? If members of your household all want to use the bathroom at the same time, consider the possibility of easing the morning or evening rush by installing a freestanding shower or washbasin in a bedroom. Do you have the luxury of space for a small connecting bathroom? If you have a separate half-bath, is there room there for a shower? Does it make sense to remove the toilet from the bathroom and locate it elsewhere to make more room?

The size and arrangement of your existing bathroom, plus the siting of windows and doors, will play a key role in how it is used. Take accurate measurements so that you know exactly what you are dealing with. Measure floor to ceiling height as well as length and breadth. Draw a rough plan and mark in doors and windows, and the current plumbing arrangements, too. It is always a good idea to have all these measurements on hand when you go shopping.

Let us start with the very smallest of bathrooms. Unless you deliberately choose a style of decor that is vivacious and incorporates hoards of curious objects, a tiny space is best kept plain and simple.

There is certainly something very satisfying about making the most of a tiny space – and plenty of inspiration can be found by looking at bathrooms on boats and houseboats as well as in campers and trailers. Clean, smooth lines, compact fixtures, built-in cabinets and light colors all open out a space. Make the most of any natural light. It may be possible to enlarge the window or, if your bathroom is at the top of the house, put in a skylight.

A large bathroom is, of course, the most flexible of all. Here you will have room to experiment and really wallow in luxury. Fit in that shower or second washbasin you have always wanted. Perhaps you can make a feature of a beautiful bathtub and place it right in the center of the room. A chair for relaxing after a bath is a must.

How will the bathroom be used?

Are you the sort of person who enjoys long, luxurious baths, or do you prefer quick, refreshing showers? Do you have a large bathroom that could accommodate a home sauna, a collection of gym equipment, a rowing machine, or an exercise bicycle?

If you have a small budget for renovating your house or apartment, there is little to be

The addition of wood textures makes a handsome bathroom. The side of the bathtub is given a painted wood-grain effect which complements the wooden chair and flooring. Added interest is given to the plain creamy walls with the checkered tile pattern.

gained by spending most of it on an expensive bathroom. If you can happily live with the existing fixtures, your time, effort, and money will be best spent smartening up the room with some new tiles, a coat of fresh paint, and good lighting. A stylish, top-quality bathroom can enhance the value of your property, but if you plan to stay in your current home for just a short time, then a large investment is unwise.

Young children, the elderly, and the disabled can bring all sorts of different needs. Children will want to be independent and use the toilet and basin by themselves. This is made easy by providing a small step on which they can stand. Someone suffering from arthritis may find ordinary faucets difficult to use, so look for types that are designed for ease of use. A wide doorway is necessary for a wheelchair user. Pay special attention at this point to finishes, too. The bathroom is furnished with hard objects that will cause injury in the case of a fall. Consider non-slip flooring and incorporate rounded edges where possible.

What would I most like to change?

This is the time to crystallize your thoughts. To be thorough, think more broadly than the good and bad elements of your own bathroom, and remember what you liked and disliked about your last bathroom and your friends' and family's bathrooms.

A good place to start is with the fixtures. Do you like the fixtures in your existing bathroom; if not, what sort of thing do you like?

Would you like a double bowl washbasin? What style of bathroom do you prefer: do you like very functional, sleek, ceramic-tiled rooms, or something softer with wood paneling on the walls, gentle lighting, carpet or cushioned vinyl, on the floor and an upholstered easy chair? If your current bathroom has built-in cabinets already, do you like the doors and handles? If not, perhaps these can be painted or replaced. Changing doors can transform a room easily and inexpensively. If you are aiming for a nautical look, then try plain pine with brass catches; if you want something a little more stream-lined, there are plenty of smooth-finished doors in all colors.

The color scheme may be dictated by the fixtures. If you have chosen to keep the existing fixtures then you may like to devise a complementary scheme. The more adventurous could try a daring contrast: sunshine yellow to go with a green or purple to offset pink. If you are unsure, neutral colors such as white and cream are a safe bet and extremely easy to live with until you feel inspired. Alternatively, if you have a dark bathroom, you might like to transform it into a light, white space; or you could play on the darkness and turn it into an intriguing, dark cavern. Do you like hot colors such as reds and oranges, or cool tones of blue and green? Do you have a favorite item – a chair, painting, or curtains – that you would like to build a color scheme around?

Once you have an idea of colors and styles, begin to think about finishes. There is a huge choice of bathroom wall coverings and floorings, and many of the options will be discussed later in this book (see page 54). In the meantime, visit plenty of showrooms, compare prices, and ask friends why they came to choose their particular flooring or wallpaper and whether they are happy with it. Ask if their finishes were easy to install, whether they are hard-wearing, and if there are any drawbacks. For example, ceramic floor tiles may look great, but they can be cold to walk on barefoot.

Lighting can be extremely difficult to get just right (see page 53). For the time being, ask yourself whether you like side lighting or a central lamp. Would ceiling-recessed fixtures be a good idea? Do you like to wash in bright, crisp light, or a slightly softer glow?

Finally, consider whether you can afford to invest in a water softener. They can be expensive to install, but will provide you with wonderfully soft water and will save many problems with mineral deposits in pipes that can stain fixtures. Also, decide what sort of heating might be appropriate and whether you need any additional ventilation to cope with moisture and mildew.

What can I achieve within my budget?

Now comes the moment of reckoning. Take your list of "likes" and mark it up in order of priority. Once you have figured out your

Drama in black and white is enhanced by the powerful pattern of Roman heads on the wallpaper and the bold floor tiles. Stainless steel details work extremely well with the monochrome decor, and crisp, white towels are a must after taking an invigorating shower.

order of works, you should make an estimate of how much you will need to spend on alterations and decorating materials.

With so many temptations in the showroom, it is very easy to overspend, so be absolutely clear about what you can afford. Make sure you build in an emergency fund of perhaps ten percent for unexpected eventualities.

If you are planning to live with this bathroom for just a short time, do not be tempted spend a fortune. Even if you are expecting to stay for five years, it is still worth considering inexpensive but effective options.

Be sure to make yourself the promise that you will shop around and compare prices. Try to get three quotations for any work to be carried out, and never take the first quote you are offered.
It is important to be well prepared, and, above all, to be realistic about what you can achieve.

Bathroom planning and design

There are few hard and fast rules in bathroom planning and design. The simple guidelines are that the room should be functional, waterproof, attractive, and comfortable.

The first consideration is the layout of your fixtures. If you have decided to keep your existing fixtures, but would like to change the arrangement, bear in mind the position of the outflow pipe. It is always a good idea to try to locate bathtub, toilet and washbasin, and therefore the pipes, along the outside wall. Of course, a straight line of bowls may not look particularly attractive, nor will it necessarily be possible to place everything along one wall; however, in general, the further you move the bathtub or toilet from the pipe, the greater the installation cost. Should it be absolutely necessary, for the purposes of your new layout, to locate the toilet a long distance away, it may be worth asking professional advice about whether it is necessary to install a macerator, an electrically-powered unit that will pump waste to its destination.

Your budget and size of room will, of course, dictate just how much reorganization you can carry out. Careful thought at this stage will save problems and expense later. Remember to refer to your notes on how you want to use the space. Always seek professional advice if you are unsure.

As you are drawing up plans, keep in mind how you and others will use the room. For example, by keeping all the fixtures in a contained area at one end or side of the room, you will free up plenty of space for storage or for a laundry area. Always make sure you leave a sensible working space around fixtures. Remember that you will need room by the side of the

bathtub for drying yourself or for kneeling to wash children. Elderly or disabled bathers may need more generous space so they can get in and out of the bathtub safely. The same guidelines apply to the washbasin, toilet, and shower. Wall-mounted safety rails can also help with safe movement around the room.

It is also important to consider the needs of those who are very tall or very short. Fixtures and built-in cabinets are designed for adults of average height. If you are very tall, one solution to the height problem is to raise the washbasin. If you are short, you could change built-in bases to lower the overall height. Also remember that mirrors will

have to be placed so that everyone can use them. The disadvantage of tailoring your bathroom so specifically is that prospective house buyers may take exception to your alterations.

To give you inspiration and help you in your planning and design, we will now discuss some ideas for three typical bathroom shapes.

The long, narrow bathroom

This shape of room almost inevitably means that you will be obliged to place your fixtures in a line. The configuration will work in almost any way: toilet, bathtub, then washbasin, or washbasin and toilet side by side followed by the bathtub. This second line-up occupies slightly less space than the former because basin and toilet can be squeezed up close. The assumption is that you will need less working space around them because they are unlikely to be used simultaneously.

If the room is very long, you may have space for a shower and/or a bidet, too. As opportunities for storage are likely to be limited, consider fitting your washbasin into a cupboard or vanity unit. If

The simplicity of this modern bathroom is achieved by dispensing with all clutter. The floor is of plain, stripped boards; the bathtub is encased in a hoop of stainless steel; and storage space is hidden by an entire wall of mirrored doors which help to reflect light and give a greater sense of space. The toilet is tucked in behind a mosaic-tiled false wall.

Bathroom planning and design

you choose to make a feature of the room's elongated shape, fit a continuous built-in line down one side to hold your fixtures, and tile walls and floor. Always make sure that there is easy maintenance access to pipes hidden by units. Decorative lines of tiles, or wallpaper borders running lengthwise through the space, will give the effect of stretching the room even longer.

If you prefer to break up the line effect, put a narrow shelf unit on the wall opposite the bathtub and basin. This could be in the form of a bookcase and is ideal for storing toiletries and plants. Also consider a wall-mounted, heated towel rod, a decorative tile mural, a large mirror, or perhaps a painting.

Another excellent idea to break up the row effect is to build in a waist-high screen at either or both ends of the bathtub. This can be tiled and will not only give you extra shelf space, but also screen the toilet. If there is space, it can be extended to ceiling height and form one side of a shower cubicle.

Where the room is wide enough, you may choose to install the washbasin or toilet at the far end. If the room is wider still, you will probably be able to place the bath widthwise across the room. This is always a very neat solution. Bathtubs are now available in many different lengths, so shop around for the size you require.

The tiny bathroom

The smallest bathrooms can also be the most efficient. There certainly will not be space to waste and, if the budget allows, you may be able to splash out on more exotic finishes – marble, for example – that you would not be able to afford to furnish a larger space. Connecting bathrooms are usually fairly compact, so this section will apply to them too.

Small-sized washbasins will gain you a little extra room, as will slim built-in cabinets and slim-line toilet cisterns. Wall-hung sinks and toilets will provide you with extra floor space.

For more substantial space gains, it may be possible to put in a smaller bathtub. Rehanging an inward-opening door to make it outward-opening will reclaim extra floor space. Could you remove the bathtub altogether and replace it with a shower? This latter suggestion deserves very careful consideration. It could slightly deter a prospective buyer if he or she is particularly partial to taking baths.

If there is no opportunity to gain more space, then clearly you must make the most of what you have. Built-in cabinets, both floor and wallmounted, will give the room a stream-lined, more spacious feel and provide valuable storage capacity. Plumbing pipes can be hidden in the walls.

Color is an important factor, too (see page 46). Light-colored rooms will appear larger than dark ones. By the same token, additional natural light in the form of a larger window or a skylight can enhance the feeling of space.

Raise the temperature with a palette of pulsating, rich, earthy colors. Unusual decoration based on Inca designs is used liberally in wall murals, borders, and on the side of the bathtub. The complex geometric patterns are echoed on the textured fabrics of the rugs and the throw over the sofa.

The square bathroom

This shape really is the ideal and provides the opportunity for many different layouts. Most bathroom designs start with the bathtub; if it is placed lengthwise against one wall and there is extra space, you may want to consider installing a separate shower or a storage cabinet to complete the run. Next, decide on positions for the toilet and washbasin. As mentioned earlier, the toilet is best placed close to the outflow pipe to make efficient drainage. The basin can be placed alongside or opposite. The door position will probably dictate the site. Make sure the door can open without crashing into the fixtures – chips and cracks can be irreparable. If you have the luxury of a generous-sized space, the bath can be turned to point into the center of the room with only the faucets end against the wall.

Space planning

Disciplined and thoughtful space planning really makes the most of any bathroom. As a general rule, a standard bath will need about 32 inches of floor space along the long side for drying yourself or for

kneeling and bathing infants; a toilet requires around 32 inches of floor space in front and 28 inches widthwise for comfortable use; a washbasin needs some 32 inches in front for bending space, and a shower will need the same in front for drying. These space allowances can overlap since it is usual for only one person at a time to use the room. If you have very young children, think about incorporating space for changing diapers. Also build in extra space to maneuver for those in wheelchairs.

Always think carefully about the positions of protruding fixtures such as toilet-paper holders and towel rods. It can be both annoying and dangerous constantly to bump into these. Once you have worked out the first draft of your plan, it is a good idea to call in the professionals for advice and quotations. It is best to enlist the help of an experienced plumber and to get at least three quotations. The cheapest will not necessarily be the best. Select a plumber whom you like, who understands your needs, and who has quoted a fair price for the job.

Ventilation

A build-up of moisture is undesirable, not just esthetically (it can produce unsightly black mildew marks), but also structurally, because it can rot and cause material damage to walls, window frames, and floors. The solution is to make sure your bathroom is adequately ventilated. This can be achieved by installing simple window vents. However, if the problem is acute, you may need

to put in an electrically-powered extractor fan; the sort recommended for bathrooms are usually activated by a pull cord and switch off automatically. A powerful ventilator is essential, and maybe required by law, in a bathroom without windows.

Storage

Take stock of all those items that you would like to store in your bathroom. You will certainly need ready-made linen storage. You may want to build in space for toiletries, cosmetics, medicines, cleaning materials, spare toilet paper, and perhaps a laundry basket.

In recent years, many manufacturers have borrowed from the excellent ideas of built-in kitchen specialists and have devised many selections of built-in bathroom furniture. These are available in a wide variety of finishes and styles, and offer all sorts of storage details such as swing-out drawers, pull-out shelving, in-built shelves, inset lighting, and laundry baskets.

At the very least, you will probably need a lockable medicine cabinet, or one that is well out of the reach of children. Some storage for toiletries and cosmetics is a good idea. How about a place for storing bathroom cleaning materials? This could be under the sink or perhaps in a place under the bathtub?

However, if you prefer a freestanding bathroom, let your imagination run riot. You may want to opt for a more random selection of cabinets and shelves.

An old sideboard will provide excellent towel storage space – paint it to match your scheme; a pine hutch or armoire will carry just about anything you could possibly need in a bathroom; bookcases can help you put everything away out of sight.

Because so many bathroom accessories and toiletries are attractive, open shelving looks great. Choose glass, wood, or even rustproof metal.

Finishes for cabinets and countertops

The finishes you choose will help to set the style of your bathroom. As a guide, if you want to create a warm, comfortable feel, then choose from a palette of natural materials, particularly woods. For an efficient, hygienic style of bathroom, select smooth finish laminates.

To transform old bathroom cabinets, it is now possible to buy and install new doors. As long as your cabinets are sound and of a standard size, this can save a great deal of unnecessary expense in buying entirely new units. You can even achieve a simple facelift just by replacing the old handles.

Countertops are available in dozens of materials, textures, and patterns. One of the most popular, practical, and least expensive is laminate. This man-made material copes well with the wear and tear of bathroom life, as it is tough, waterproof, hygienic, and scratch- and stain-resistant. More expensive man-made materials include Corian, a

The light fittings around this glamorous dressing-room style mirror are watertight and specially designed for use in bathrooms. For the ultimate luxury you could install a heated mirror, which would not steam up.

type of artificial stone. Like laminate, it is hard-wearing, easily wiped clean, and water- and heat-resistant. Unlike laminate, it is a solid material that can be cut and shaped to provide a smooth and seamless surface.

Woods such as beech and maple have an enduring appeal and are easily cut to the required size and shape. When they are oiled or varnished, they are water-resistant, but require some maintenance to keep them looking good. If you look after it properly, wood will improve with age. Always check the source of the wood you are buying – imported hardwoods may have been cut from rain forests or other unsustainable sources.

Planning Tips

• Always use qualified plumbers and electricians.

• A small step allows young children to reach and use the washbasin safely. Make sure, however, that they cannot use it to reach medicines which should be kept in a locked cabinet. Cleaning materials must be kept well out of reach of children, too.

• Only use electrical appliances and switches recommended for use in the bathroom.

• Keep all electrical appliances well away from water.

• Consider installing hand grips or rails to make it easier for the young, elderly, and disabled to get in and out of the bathtub.

• A small plastic stool or flap-down seat can make it easier for the young and the elderly to enjoy a shower in comfort.

• When looking for showers, check that the one you have chosen has in-built temperature stabilization or thermostatic control. This is particularly important if young children are going to use the shower as it will prevent them

from being scalded or chilled.

• Dripping faucets waste water and can cause mineral deposits – replace the washers immediately.

• It is now possible to buy mirrors that contain a heating element to prevent them from misting.

• Always check your local building regulations before making major alterations to rooms and plumbing. Your plans may require special approval.

• To cut down on heating bills, insulate your hot water tank with a jacket that is at least 3 inches thick. Line walls behind radiators with silver foil to reflect heat back into the room and turn your central heating and hot water thermostat down a degree or two.

Bathroom color

Bathroom decoration spans the entire gamut, from the sleek, white-tiled cube to the fantastic and frivolous. The style you choose is an opportunity to express your personality, although there may be compromises to make if you have decided to refurbish your bathroom around your old fixtures, rather than completely revamp the room.

You may have a very clear idea in mind of how your bathroom should look. Will it be highly decorated with floral tile and fabric patterns, in the Victorian manner? Based around a black and white check pattern, popular in 1930s Art Deco rooms? Or perhaps a mysterious watery grotto in dark greens and blues?

The secret of a successful decorative scheme is attention to detail. For example, the smartness of a high-tech bathroom will be utterly destroyed by hanging floral curtains at the window. Venetian blinds or window shades will look much more effective. Make sure all your fixtures are in matching colors – brass faucets and a chrome mirror frame will do both a disservice and spoil the effect.

Before you start any decoration work, check that all your surfaces are sound. Flaking paint should be rubbed with sandpaper, cracks, and holes should be filled, and loose tiles refixed. Old and discolored grouting can be dug out and replaced. For tiles in wet areas, buy a water-resistant grout – it is more expensive, but the investment is well worthwhile.

Wall coverings

Ceramic tiles: These are by far the most popular wall covering found in the bathroom. They are available in countless shapes, colors, and patterns, are easy to apply and offer a durable, water- and stain-resistant, bright, easy-to-clean finish. In the right setting, even the humble, square white tile can look stunning.

Their main drawback is that the grout tends to pick up stains. Scrubbing in between tiles with an old toothbrush will remove most discoloration, and there are now products on the market devised specifically for lifting off dirt. However, if stains persist, it is advisable to scrape out old grout and replace it with new.

Tiles can be used in a multitude of different ways to create the look you want. You may choose one plain color or an elaborately patterned effect. An unusual and interesting pattern can be created by mixing up an assortment of plain or plain and patterned tiles. For a really eyecatching effect, set square tiles on their points to form a diamond shape. Mosaics, many of which are sold in ready-assembled panels, are unusual and stylish used on both walls and floors.

If you choose to tile the side of your bathtub or walls and panels that enclose pipes or the toilet tank, make sure you can gain access for maintenance. This is achieved either by tiling an entire panel and then grouting it into place, or by tiling a panel and setting it in place with round-head mirror screws. Always buy a few spare tiles in case of damage during installation or for future repairs.

Wood paneling: Kits for wood paneling are now stocked by many hardware stores. You can opt for square panels or a tongue-and-groove style. This sort of finish works well when mounted from floor to ceiling, or from floor to counter height to give you a half-paneled room. The wood is usually sold unfinished so you can choose whether to varnish or paint it.

If you are feeling adventurous, you may consider searching out old, reclaimed wood paneling from an architectural salvage yard. Carefully chosen items can look extremely handsome in a bathroom.

Wallpaper: This is a popular choice in bathrooms since it can soften the hardness of sanitaryware and ceramic tiles. Due to the inevitability of condensation and water splashes in the bathroom, it is always wise to choose vinyl paper which is coated with a water-resistant seal as it will last longer and can be sponged clean.

The complete antithesis of the surgically pristine white-tiled shower, this colorful cubicle will set the pulse racing and has plenty of room for a vigorous scrub to start the day.

Paint: A coat of paint is often all that is needed to transform a bathroom. Walls must be sound and free from damp, flaking paint and peeling wallpaper. While paint, especially oil-based, is durable, it is not recommended for wall areas most exposed to water – such as those directly above the bathtub, by the shower, or behind the washbasin.

When it comes to applying the paint, if you want to be adventurous, you could try a mural or any one of the many paint effects that have become so popular in recent years. Dozens of books have been published with step-by-step instructions on such techniques as rag rolling, sponging, and dragging. Stippling is a particularly effective finish. Of course, among the most popular of paint decoration effects is stenciling. There are numerous specialist companies producing a vast array of stencil designs – from simple flowers, sea creatures, and shells to complex and intricate effects – which are available, complete with full instructions, from good craft, hardware, and department stores. Once again, check the instructions to make sure the paint you choose is suitable for use in the bathroom.

Color schemes

Once you have chosen a decorative theme, you can start to make some

decisions about the colors you would like. You will certainly have thought long and hard about schemes and may have made some color decisions already by choosing the fixtures. Selecting the colors for walls, ceiling and woodwork is great fun. If ever you are unsure about a color, buy a few test cans and experiment with different looks.

Personal preference and association are powerful ingredients in making your choice. If you have fond memories of a childhood bathroom, for example, you may want to create a similar color

This bathroom is decorated with shells and other interesting textured accessories in soft, natural colors to give a relaxing look.

scheme. If you do not have a particular color in mind, it is a good idea to build a scheme around some stunning tiles you have discovered, reclaimed wood paneling, a favorite painting, or perhaps a suitable theme such as the beach.

In practical terms, you should take into account the colors of the items already chosen: blues, yellows, and white, for example, look wonderful with natural wood finishes; blue and white are clean and crisp; black and white looks extremely chic with white fixtures; dark blue is rich and handsome; black is sexy, and so on.

Take careful note of the natural light in your room. North-facing bathrooms may receive no direct sunlight; east-facing rooms receive the weak morning sun; west-facing bathrooms will get the rich evening light, while those that are south-facing will receive direct sunlight through most of the day. To make a room feel warmer, choose from the red end of the spectrum, or choose soft neutrals such as cream and ivory. For a cooler effect, use blues and greens.

It is possible to improve the quality of light by replacing old obscured glass with clear or slightly tinted panes. This, however, is only recommended if your bathroom is not overlooked. Should you have eagle-eyed neighbors, consider replacing the thick, old glass with a modern etched pane. Etching gives a soft, pale, frosted effect; a good glazier will be able to etch the glass for you. A decorative stained-glass window will also deter any onlookers and can provide an intriguing, colorful, and attractive focus for the room.
A badly room may look its best simply in white – white does, in fact, suit almost every bathroom because of its associations with cleanliness, hygiene, and purity.

Bathroom fixtures

When making your decisions, it is always a good idea to try out the items for size and comfort. You may feel a little foolish lying flat out in an empty bath in the showroom, but it is well worth the temporary embarrassment to find one that is really comfortable. Sit on the toilet and imagine washing in the basin. Every piece has its own distinctive shape and peculiarities; make sure they work with your own body. It would be a terrible mistake to spend a small fortune buying and installing bathroom fixtures, only to discover that you knocked your elbow on the sculpted armrest of the bath every time you got in and out.

The bathtub

The bathtub has undergone a massive personality change since the era of the tin tub. In the early days, it was a purely functional receptacle that was hauled in front of the fire once a week for a quick wash. It was hardly the place to enjoy a long, lingering soak.

Your main considerations when buying a bathtub are the size you need, the shape and style, the comfort factor, the position and type of faucet holes, and the material from which it is made. The size should be evident from your plan; however, you will be offered a choice of different internal shapes. Try them out; they will vary in depth, width, length, and contours. If you enjoy a soak in really deep water, check the height of the overflow outlet. Special shapes – bathtubs with low sides, for example – are designed for the elderly or disabled.

If you have the good fortune to be looking for new bathroom fixtures, be prepared to be spoiled for choice. During recent years, manufacturers have produced collections in every style imaginable. Whether your taste is for a decorative Victorian bathroom, angular Art Deco, frivolous shell shapes, sleek high tech, or for the most recent, smooth, rounded, ergonomically formed shapes, with a little hunting around, you are sure to be able to find a set to suit you.

Think carefully before you buy; bathroom fixtures can be very expensive. It is also worth checking the weight of items, especially cast-iron bathtubs, to make sure that your floors can take the strain. Also, if you opt for a wall-hung toilet, make sure your walls are strong enough.

A good selection of easy-to-operate faucets is now on offer, as are all shapes and sizes of grab rails to make it easy to get in and out of the bathtub.

The style you buy is entirely up to you. Do you want a period look, a freestanding bathtub with exposed feet, a sunken bath (only realistic for ground-floor bathrooms), or something that can be enclosed? If you are looking for a genuine cast-iron Victorian period article, try an architectural salvage yard if there is one in your town or city. Before parting with your cash, check it inside and out very carefully for scratches, chips, and cracks. It is possible to repair small dents and to have the bathtub resurfaced, but serious flaws, cracks especially, are terminal.

If you would like a bathtub with an overhead shower, consider the shapes that have a flat, slightly squared-off bed at the shower end –

this makes it a great deal easier and safer to use the shower. Check on types that incorporate non-slip surfaces. Or, perhaps your heart is set on a corner-fitting bath? They take up slightly more room than the regular rectangular shape; make sure you have allowed for the difference in your plans.

If your budget allows, you have the option to buy bathtubs with integrated whirlpools and spa features, sold with the claim that they will gently massage and tone aching muscles and joints. While the medical profession may reserve judgment on the actual physical benefits, few can deny that a bathtub full of swirling, frothing water is fun and can make you feel great. This type of tub is available in a choice of three different actions: the whirlpool, which simply recirculates the bath water; spa baths, which pump air through water; and the whirlpool spa, which pumps a mixture of air and water.

The classic Victorian-style roll-top bathtub and pedestal sink remain perennial favorites. They are generous in size and always look stylish. The handsome bathtub is given pride of place and becomes the main focus of the room. Pretty mosaic tiles provide decorative panels on the otherwise plain walls.

Take care in making your choice to make sure the model meets safety regulations and enlist the help of an expert for installation.

The style of the faucets will depend on your taste, but remember to make sure that the bathtub and faucets are compatible. Some bathtubs are sold with three holes for faucets and a central spout; some are sold with just one hole for a monobloc (a single spout with handles attached at the sides), and some have no holes and are intended for those bathrooms that have faucets and spout mounted on the wall. You might consider a bathtub with a central or corner mounted faucet area and plug hole.

Bathtubs are available in several materials as follows:

Acrylic: This material is extremely popular; it will not rust or corrode and is very light. Acrylic baths are vacuum-formed from a thin sheet of material that is usually reinforced underneath with glass fiber. The thicknesses can range from around ¼ inch up to ½ inch. These bathtubs have the additional advantages of being warm to the touch; they keep water warmer for longer and are easily wiped clean.

Steel: This is tough and hardwearing and coated with porcelain or vitreous enamel. The steel used for bathtubs is usually between ⅛ inch and ¼ inch thick. For the most rigid structure, buy the thickest that you can afford.

Cast iron: A very heavy and hardwearing material, cast iron is usually coated in a softer enamel than those used on steel. Abrasive cleaners should not be used on this type of bath. The disadvantage of cast iron is that the water in the bath cools rapidly.

The toilet

Just about all toilets are now made in vitreous china. This is a tough, hardwearing, stain-resistant material, but it can chip and may even crack if it gets a hefty knock.

The main consideration when choosing a toilet is whether you would like a wall- or floor-mounted model. As mentioned earlier, the wall-mounted version frees floor space but, because it is heavy and can weigh around 40 pounds, it should be mounted on a strong wall.

The variety of styles matches that on offer for bathtubs. Take note of the position of the tank as this can be crucial to your efficient use of room; there are space- and water-saving options. Victorian-style models have a high-level tank and the flush is operated by a pull chain. The more modern tanks fit directly behind the bowl and are operated by a handle. These tanks are available in a variety of designs: there are those where the tank is left on show and others where it is designed to be concealed in a box with the pipes. It is also possible to buy very slim-line tanks that can fit into the depth of a wall; these are extremely water efficient.

The wash basin

Like the toilet, these are almost always made in vitreous china. Basins are available in all sorts of shapes and sizes, from corner-fitted models, square, oval and round pedestal or wall-hung types, to those which fit or are semi-inset into vanity units.

You can get some washbasins that are formed in a continuous piece with wide counter areas on each side and others which come as freestanding wash stands. If you can afford the space, it is usually best to get a really large basin, and a shallow bowl will help you save on water consumption.

The shower

This is the most cost- and energy-efficient way of staying clean. A shower can use just one quarter of the water required to fill a tub.

When you are looking at showers, check that the controls are easy to read and to understand. Consider what sort of doors or screens are best for your bathroom.

If water pressure is low, it is best to install a shower with pump; check this with your plumber. Also, ask if you need a water-storage tank.

It is advisable to hire a professional installer and to make sure the unit is completely waterproof. Shower water is extremely invasive; it can wear away grout and will find many means of escape. Unless the water is contained, it will cause damaging mildew and rot.

If you are buying a shower for the first time, the choice can be bewildering. There are three main choices for position: over the bath, in a tiled cubicle, or in a freestanding shower unit.

Next comes the type of system. These are grouped under three main headings:

Electricity or gas: This is the most economical option. First, the units are quick and easy to install as they are simply connected to the cold-water system. Second, hot water is instantaneous as it is heated as it passes through the shower unit; this means you do not need to heat up an entire tank of water and that you can have hot showers when the rest of your hot water system is switched off.

The disadvantage of this type of shower is that it is slower to work when the weather is cold because it takes longer to heat up the incoming cold water. As a general rule, the higher the kilowatt rating (this is usually between 7.5 kW and 9 kW), the higher the flow rate.

Most shower systems are now available with multifunction shower heads that allow you to regulate the flow of water. If you live in a hard-water area, it is also worth checking to see if the head is resistant to mineral deposits or, at the very least, easily cleaned.

M i x e r: This has a higher flow rate than the electric or gas shower, as the mixer draws from both the hot and cold household supplies and then mixes them for you. It can be more costly to install

than the electric shower and relies on hot water being available at the time when you want to shower, but it is probably the most popular option. With the addition of a pump to boost the flow rate, you can turn your mixer into a power shower (see below).

Make sure the mixer control knob is easy to use and read. Some have separate controls to regulate flow and temperature. The temperature control can be very useful to prevent scalding, as it should keep the water temperature constant within a degree or two no matter what other faucets are switched on in the house. A normal flow will be between approximately 2 and 3 gallons per minute. The most powerful will pump up to 4 gallons per minute.

P o w e r: This is a pump-assisted mixer shower. It draws both hot and cold from the household supply and uses more water than either the electric or mixer types. If you are considering installing one of these, make sure the drain hole in your shower tray can cope with the volume of water that this type of shower will generate and that it is kept free of obstructions.

The power shower, although more expensive to install and run, is the ultimate in luxurious and exhilarating showering, and you can finetune the flow of water from gentle, frothy champagne bubbles to tingling needle jets. The experience can be enhanced by the addition of body sprays positioned in the wall.

The shower enclosure

Shower curtains are very reasonably priced, they are available in many attractive designs, and they can work well if they are used properly. However, unless they are thoroughly cleaned and dried on a regular basis, they can become slimy and mildewed. Some types of curtain can be washed in the washing machine.

Currently, the most popular choice for the shower enclosure is a screen or door. Screens are manufactured in glass or acrylic; avoid materials with ridges which will harbor dirt. Make sure they form a watertight fit with the top of your bathtub (especially roll tops) or shower tray. They are easy to clean and durable. If you choose a folding screen, make sure that it folds inward to prevent water from dripping on the floor.

The same attention to water tightness applies to shower cubicles. Make sure all joints are sealed and that doors fit closely.

The shower tray

For the freestanding shower, a good, solid tray is essential. Most trays are manufactured in either ceramic or acrylic, and the most popular are square shaped. Some are made with a small up-stand which fits against the wall and provides a watertight seal with the surrounding tiles. Trays need to be completely rigid and must be laid on a solid base to prevent any movement. If you choose an acrylic model, check that it does not move – this is easily achieved by standing in the tray and rocking from foot to foot. It should also have adjustable feet so that it can be laid level.

If you opt to buy a tailor-made shower enclosure, make sure it is compatible with the tray.

The bidet

Bidets are becoming increasingly popular and, like toilets and washbasins, are usually made in vitreous china. They can be wall or floor-hung. If you choose a wall-mounted model, make sure your wall is strong enough to support the unit.

The water arrives in a choice of three ways: an under-rim supply which flows down the side of the bowl, an ascending spray, or an over-rim supply. The latter resembles a regular mixer faucet and is the most popular.

The faucets

Just like bathroom fixtures, these come in every conceivable style: the old-fashioned cross-head shape, laboratory-style lever operated, acrylic-capped pillar taps, bath/shower mixers, three piece mixers, and monoblocs. You can buy single-stem units, wall-hung faucets and Victorian-style "telephone" units, incorporating faucets, bath/shower lever, and shower head.

Some faucets are specially designed to make them easy to use and particularly suitable for the elderly or disabled. Faucets are available in many finishes: chrome, nickel, brass, gold. Be sure to choose one that will match your other bathroom accessories, and always check that your faucets are compatible with your bathtub or basin.

The lovely rounded forms of the faucet and spigot complement the shape of this washbasin.

Types of lighting

Tungsten: This is the light provided by regular household bulbs. It is also available in strips. These make excellent bathroom lighting as the unit is sealed and protected from moisture.

Fluorescent: Fluorescent tubes are long-lasting and energy-efficient and therefore cheap to run. Ideally, this type of lighting should be installed behind a shield.

Halogen: This is low-voltage and emits a wonderful, crisp, white, sparkling light. This type of lighting has become increasingly popular in recent years and is now available in a variety of styles. The bulbs are sold as spotlights, which cast a small pool of concentrated light, or wide angle, which shed larger pools with softer edges.

Do bear in mind that the installation of halogen lights is a specialist task since they need transformers. These are usually in the form of small boxes or tubes, and they transform the powerful voltage into a low-voltage supply. They can either be placed close to the light source or remotely. They usually emit a slight hum, and so are best placed inside the ceiling recess or, perhaps, a cabinet.

Lighting Design

You will need two types of lighting. First, an overall room light, and second, task lights over the washbasin and mirror. Separate switches are advisable. When choosing lighting for a bathroom, remember that bulbs should not be

Bathroom lighting

Water and electricity are a very dangerous combination and, therefore, any work carried out on bathroom lighting should be completed by a professional. It is also important to formulate your ideas about lighting schemes and plan ahead before you start work on a task such as wall tiling, as the wires should be traced into the wall. Good lighting is always a wise investment. It can enhance the room's decor and help create its atmosphere. The wrong type of lighting will drastically reduce your enjoyment of the room. It would be a terrible shame to spoil all your hard work by installing inappropriate lights.

exposed to condensation. An overhead fixture rarely adds anything to a bathroom unless it is adequately supplemented by wall lights and task lights. It can shed a rather stark light and will cause shadows. Fluorescent is not ideal either; it is harsh and unflattering.

For a softer, all-round glow, consider wall lights. Choose fixtures to suit the rest of your decor and mount them above eye level to give a gentle, inviting glow. This sort of lighting works extremely well with pale color schemes and natural materials such as wood and cork. Remember that dark colors absorb light and will probably need more light fixtures than reflective white or pale color schemes.

For dramatic, sparkly lighting, take a look at the choice of ceiling-recessed fixtures. Recessed tungsten and low-voltage halogen lights complement fresh and bright colors and lots of ceramic tiling. Some have a movable "eyeball" center that can be directed to wash a wall with light or to highlight specific objects or areas.

Recessed lights are a good idea in bathrooms with low ceilings and can be bought in watertight units. If you have a high ceiling, an excellent way of throwing light up is to mount small uplighters above wall cabinets or on high shelves. Light will bounce off the ceiling and fall as a soft glow.

For basin and mirror task lighting, small strips of tungsten work well. These can be placed behind baffles to prevent glare. Low-voltage halogen is also excellent and, because of its pure, crisp light, will make chrome, glass, and ceramic really sparkle. For the ultimate in glitz and glamor, you could opt for a dressing room-style mirror framed by globe light bulbs.

Last, do not forget candles. Although it is not practical for everyday lighting, candlelight is difficult to beat, especially for a really relaxing, soothing soak.

Bathroom flooring

Bathrooms, especially family ones, are subjected to tremendous wear and tear, and the flooring you choose must be tough and, above all, waterproof or equipped with efficient drainage. Even where money is no object, some finishes, such as stone, may be out of the question because your floor simply cannot take the weight. Very heavy materials should only be laid on a solid concrete floor, or there is a danger of causing structural damage. Ceramic and terracotta tiles are also best laid on a solid floor, partly because of their weight but also because, if they are laid on a wood base, the joints will move and crack. It is sensible to check with a builder or supplier if you are considering one of these types of flooring.

Your choice of color and pattern is also important. A plain-colored floor, especially if it is white, will show every mark. A flecked design or small pattern will spare you hours of cleaning. That said, floors with a light-colored base will brighten a room, while darker shades will close it in.

Lively patterns can overwhelm a bathroom. If you are lucky enough to have a large room, it could look stunning with a bold black and white checkerboard design, whereas this treatment could completely overpower a small bathroom. In smaller spaces, a plain finish is generally preferable: so, if in doubt, keep it simple.

Types of flooring

Wood: If you are lucky enough to have good floorboards, you can have a marvelous stripped and varnished floor at a very reasonable cost.

Wood is durable, chic, and warm, and can improve with age; however,
it can be dented and scar and, unless it is thoroughly sealed with a durable varnish (yacht varnish is the most watertight), it may not wear well if regularly doused with water. It is a good idea to use a mat beside the bathtub or shower to soak up most of the water. Also, wood is not particularly good at sound-proofing, and it needs some maintenance such as occasional revarnishing.

You will probably need to replace some damaged boards and rent a professional sanding machine to lift off the worn and grubby top surface. If new boards are a lighter color than your existing ones, you can "age" them by painting on a couple of coats of cold, black tea or by using a wood stain. For a pickled effect, paint the sanded boards with watered-down white latex and then protect with flat varnish. You could even decorate the floor with stencils or colored wood stains. When painting or varnishing floors, make sure you start at the corner farthest from the door.

If all this sounds like too much effort, a good-quality wood finish is possible with the wood veneer and laminate packs available in hardware stores. The laminate finish is virtually indestructible, and there is a good choice of styles and colors – from prepared wood "tiles" (small wood strips mounted on a backing material) to lengths of tongue-and-groove.

The secret of achieving a professional finish is to make sure your existing floor is completely flat and firm. Most of the "do-it yourself" packs are best set on a layer of sturdy blockboard or masonite. When working on any sort of wood flooring for the bathroom, always make sure the joints are completely sealed – water can cause serious damage.

Vinyl: This incredibly tough material is stain resistant, waterproof, easy to wash clean, and warm to the touch. It is available in a wide choice of thicknesses and prices. As a general rule, the thicker it is, the more it costs.

Vinyl flooring is available either in sheet or tile form, cushioned or solid. It is manufactured in a vast array of finishes, including marble and granite effects, with decorative borders and special patterned inserts. Some manufacturers offer a design and installation service, so your floor can be tailor-made.

To achieve the best results with this material, it is essential to start with a well-prepared, flat base – blockboard or masonite are ideal. Both tiles and sheets are easy to lay using a recommended adhesive, and are virtually maintenance-free.

Cork tiles are a perfect choice for a bathroom floor. They are warm underfoot and hard-wearing, provided they have been sealed to make them water-resistant. If you lay natural tiles, you can stain them to match the bathroom scheme.

Linoleum: This finish shares many of the properties of vinyl. It is warm, stain resistant, durable, easily washable, and is also available in sheet or tile form. In recent years, linoleum has enjoyed a revival because it is manufactured with natural materials such as cork, linseed oil, wood, and resins. As demand has increased, so has the choice of colors and patterns.

Cork tiles: Easy to clean, warm underfoot, inexpensive, tough, easy to lay, and with an intriguing, mottled finish, cork has remained popular for years. It has the added advantage of being a natural substance that is grown as a renewable material.

Tiles are sold preprepared with a vinyl coating, or in their natural state. The natural tiles are slightly easier to cut and fit to awkward shapes and may then be colored. Cork tiles should be laid on a dry, flat surface, and thorough sealing is essential to provide resistance to water and long life. Use a mat in front of the bathtub or shower to soak up most of the water.

Ceramic tiles: The choice of ceramic tiles is enormous and includes hundreds of beautiful colors and patterns. Tiles are hardwearing, easily cleaned, and

are available in price ranges to suit almost all budgets, however, they are hard, cold underfoot, and noisy. They also become slippery when wet, which is not good news in the bathroom; however, some slip-resistant finishes are available.

Almost without exception, ceramic tiles should be laid on solid floors, as they are likely to be too heavy to be laid on top of sprung wood floors. For the very best results, especially in large areas, these tiles should be laid professionally.

Hard finishes: Stone, slate, and marble can look gorgeous. Stone acquires a glorious patina with age; slate has a sleek, understated grandeur; and marble can look incredibly luxurious. All are very hardwearing and rather expensive too. They are also hard, cold, and tend to be noisy.

Lightweight marble and slate slips or tiles are increasingly available and are a much cheaper option than the heavier slabs.

Terrazzo: An aggregate composed of stone and glass chips and concrete, terrazzo is tough, colorful, and available in tiles or slabs. Terrazzo is best laid on solid floors because of its heavy weight; and it is worth paying an expert to fit it.

Carpet: Carpet is warm and soft underfoot and available in extensive choices. If you decide on carpet, you should always buy a quality recommended for use in the bathroom.

Project 6

Decorating plain tiles

This is a quick and simple way of brightening up old, plain tiles. Paint on a pattern or, if you have children, let them make up their own designs. You will find everything you need to do this at a good art and craft store.

Tools and Materials

- masking tape
- old newspapers
- drawing paper
- a selection of brightly-colored ceramic paints
- 2 or 3 watercolor paintbrushes
- clear ceramic varnish

1 Make sure the tiles are clean. Wash them with a bathroom cleaner or liquid detergent and rinse well. Let the tiles dry thoroughly before you start work.

2 Using the masking tape and newspaper, mask off the wall directly around the tiles to protect it from misdirected paint spatters. Also cover the faucets and basin.

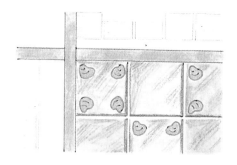

3 Work out the designs on sheets of paper. They can, of course, be as simple or as complex as you like. You could try a small mural – waves, Noah's ark, sea creatures, a shipwreck – or a series of designs for individual tiles featuring boats, fishes, sea horses, shells, and so on. Once you have the outline of the shapes, and the pattern, choose the colors of each image. The proportion of the design to the area being painted is important. Create a design which is not going to be too overpowering.

Freestyle painting is not difficult — you just need confidence and a steady hand. Have a rag handy to wipe away any shapes which do not work the first time.

4 Carefully paint the designs on to the tiles. Work from left to right if you are right-handed, and from right to left if you are left-handed; this means that you will not smudge the wet paint as you work. Let it dry thoroughly.

5 To protect the paintings from water splashes, seal the surface with a coat of clear ceramic varnish.

Project 7

Painting a wall frieze

A colorful frieze is easy to paint and inexpensive, and can look dazzling. Try stenciling a pattern or, for added charm, hand drawing your own designs.

Tools and Materials

- pencil
- stencils
- masking tape
- ¼ in and ½ in watercolor brushes or stencil brushes
- latex or stencil paint suitable for bathrooms

1 For the best results, set aside plenty of time for thorough preparation. Make sure the wall surface is smooth and sound – take care to remove any flaking paint and glue any wallpaper joints that may have come unstuck. Use filler to repair any holes and sand to a smooth finish.

2 For both a hand-drawn and a stenciled border, mark with a pencil the area to be decorated. If you plan to give the frieze a colored background, this is the time to do that. Let the paint dry before moving on to the next stage.

3 In the case of a hand-drawn design, it is a good idea to pencil in the entire outline to act as a painting guide. This will also give you the opportunity to see the design and make adjustments before you start applying paint. Avoid the temptation to try extremely complex designs – simple can also be effective. A light pencil outline will be adequate – heavy lines may prove difficult to cover or remove. For stencils, lightly pencil mark where the stencil pattern will appear.

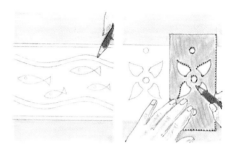

4 When you are happy with your design, you can start painting. For hand-drawn designs, work from left to right if you are right-handed to avoid smudging your work. Allow plenty of time for paint to dry before laying another color on top. When stenciling, hold the stencil in place with masking tape as you paint. Paint should be applied sparingly to avoid smudging. Remove the stencil carefully from the wall and wipe away any excess paint from the back before sticking it on the wall again.

Once the paint has dried, you can protect the frieze from water splashes with a coat of clear varnish.

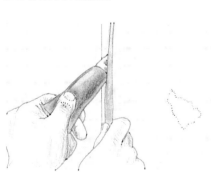

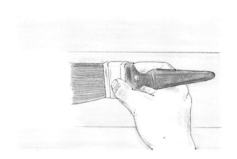

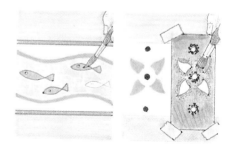

Project 8

Making a wooden slat mat

A wooden slat mat makes an unusual and practical feature in the bathroom. You won't have to stand around on cold floors when you get out of the shower or bathtub. And the natural wood looks great as part of a seaside or boat theme.

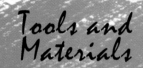

Tools and Materials

- ½ x 4 in pine boards — lengths required are 2 x 20½ in and 4 x 30 in
- wood glue
- ¾ in screws
- clear varnish

1 Sand the boards to make sure they are smooth and splinter-free. Take the four 30-inch pieces and lay them side by side, leaving a space between each of approximately 1½ inches. On top of them and at right angles, lay the two 20½-inch lengths of wood approximately 14 inches apart. Mark their positions in pencil.

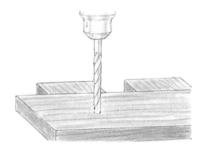

2 The screws are to be driven into the 20½ inch pieces. When the slat mat is complete, these form the base. Mark their positions in pencil. To make sure the screws go into the wood easily and do not protrude and damage the floor, it is a good idea to start the hole with a drill to the depth of a fraction of an inch.

3 Before you insert the screws, lay all the lengths of wood in place and glue. Once the glue has dried, secure the slats with the screws, one to each slat.

4 To complete the slat mat, check that all screw heads are sunk below the wood surface and sand the entire unit. You can opt to paint the finished article - making sure you give it a coat of wood primer before adding the gloss or eggshell paint, or, as shown in our pictures, add flat or gloss varnish to seal the wood and show off the natural grain.

Project 9

Paneling in the bathroom

A classic in bathroom design, tongue-and-groove paneling looks fabulous, and it is also an excellent way to hide ugly pipes and disguise old tiles or uneven walls. Rooms are usually paneled either from floor to dado height, or from floor to ceiling.

Tongue-and-groove is surprisingly easy to install and comes in a variety of materials and finishes; among the most versatile is pine - it can be painted or varnished any color you choose. Measure your bathroom carefully.

Tools and Materials

- 2 x 2 inch softwood battens (buy larger battens if you are paneling over pipe work that protrudes more than 2 inches.
- plumb line or spirit level
- screws or nails
- hammer
- sufficient tongue-and-groove paneling
- lost-head nails
- paint or varnish

1 Remove the baseboard and the dado – these can be replaced later, if desired.

2 Attach the battens to the wall. If the wall is uneven, you will need to use extra pieces of thin wood or masonite behind the batten to keep it level and straight. Use a carpenter's level when mounting battens - good attention to detail at this stage will give the best possible finish. If you are mounting the boards vertically, the battens are set horizontally. It is best to leave a small gap - about 1-2 inches from the floor and ceiling - when mounting top and bottom battens. If you nail boards too close to the end, the wood may split. Position the battens at intervals of about 20-24 inches.

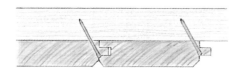

3 Starting at the left side of the wall (alternatively, if you have boards which are sold with metal clips, see Step 4), place the first board with its groove facing left. Use a plumb line or level to make sure it is completely vertical. Through the face of the board, screw or nail into position, sinking the head of the screw so that the hole can be filled and disguised. Once the first board is straight and secure, slot in the next. All subsequent boards can be set in place with invisible nailing - lost-head nails are hammered into the tongue at an angle, as shown. As their name implies, these nails can be knocked completely into the wood allowing the next board to fit neatly over the tongue.

4 Some packs of tongue-and-groove boards are sold with metal clips. To use these, you must mount the boards with the tongue facing to the left. The first, corner board must have the tongue sawn or planed off so that it will fit firmly against the wall. The clips then slot into the groove and hold the next board in place.

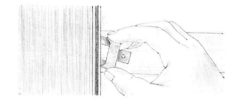

5 If the paneling covers pipes, it is usually a good idea to make it possible to remove a couple of boards for maintenance. To achieve this, saw or plane off the tongues (this makes them easy to lift out) from a couple of boards and set them in place using screws. Sink the screw heads a fraction of an inch beneath the surface of boards and fill the holes with wood putty.

6 Complete the job by replacing the baseboard, if desired, and finish with the chosen paint or varnish.

Project 10

Glass effects

This is a simply brilliant way of giving plain glass in a window or a door a frosted look, which will provide privacy in the bathroom without excluding natural light. It is even possible to add a simple stenciled pattern after the frosting is complete. The design could pick up decorative details from elsewhere in the bathroom, or be a new element in its own right.

Tools and Materials

- soapy water
- denatured alcohol
- flat or eggshell varnish
- gloss or eggshell paint
- paintbrush
- stencil and stencil brush

1 Prepare the plain glass surface by scraping off any paint or varnish splashes that may have ended up on the pane. Then, with soapy water, thoroughly wash the area to be painted. When dry, wipe over with denatured alcohol on a soft, lint-free cotton cloth so that the area is free of all dust and fibers.

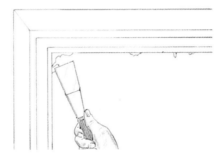

2 To make the "frosting" mix ten parts of clear flat or eggshell varnish with one part of the chosen gloss or eggshell paint color. It is obviously best to use a pale tint so that light is not obscured from the bathroom. Paint it on the glass in a light, even coat. Let it dry completely.

3 To apply the stencil pattern, use undiluted gloss or eggshell paint and apply sparingly to avoid runs and splashes.

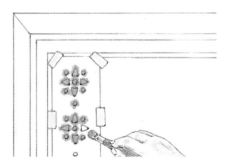

4 Carefully peel off the stencil and allow the paint to dry. If the stencil is to be used repeatedly, make sure to wipe the back clean of paint smears before re-applying it with masking tape.

Chapter three

Your kitchen

Just like successful cooking, the secret of making a perfect kitchen is in the preparation and planning. The first step is to buy a nice thick writing pad and a pencil; a large folder for all the catalogs you are sure to collect is also a good idea. Now you are equipped, take a long hard look at your kitchen – its shape, height, size, and fixtures. Then ask yourself lots of questions about what you want to keep and what you will change.

What sort of space do I have to work with?

The size and plan of your kitchen will play a key role in how it is used; take accurate measurements so that you know exactly what you are dealing with. Measure floor-to-ceiling height as well as length and breadth. Draw a rough plan and mark in doors and windows and the current plumbing arrangements, too. It is always a good idea to have all these measurements on hand when you go shopping as they can help sales staff give you appropriate advice; you never know, you might see the perfect tiles on sale and you can buy them there and then.

Starting with the very smallest of kitchens, a tiny space is best kept plain and simple unless you delight in chaos. You will need the basics, but try not to cram too much in; it will only make cooking difficult, frustrating, and even dangerous.

Remember, a small space does not have to be dull, and it can be fun to use and also extremely efficient. If you have ever taken a vacation on a houseboat or yacht, you will know

just how little space is actually needed to make a perfectly functional kitchen area. If you have a really small space to work with, it may prove useful to find and visit companies that supply kitchen appliances for boats.

Another option is to buy one of the kitchen-in-a-box units available on the market. These are the size of a closet and contain an entire mini-kitchen. The doors open out to reveal the neat arrangement of stainless steel sink, two burners, refrigerator, coffee maker, and a couple of cabinets. One upscale kitchen manufacturer has also devised an all-in-one unit which is a freestanding stainless steel bench incorporating sink, work surface, and burners. Both of these compact kitchens can be simply hooked up to the utilities and can go with you when you move.

When working with a small area, it is important to make the most of any natural light; it may even be possible to enlarge the window to open up the space more. Removing doors is always a good way of making extra space. Remember,

however, in the interests of hygiene, you should keep any doors separating kitchens and bathrooms. Perhaps knocking down a wall is an option. It may be possible to link the kitchen with the dining room or living room with an arch or widened doorway, or to knock through a serving hatch.

A medium-sized kitchen, say approximately 9 x 9 feet, will have room for a small table or fold-away breakfast bar. This sort of space is great for informal suppers, but probably not roomy enough for larger dinner parties.

The positioning of doors and windows will have a bearing on where you place cabinets or pieces of furniture. The most useful layouts work on the principal of the sink being linked to the stove on the longest, unbroken stretch of work surface. This gives you a large area for food preparation and for stacking pans and dishes for washing. The refrigerator can be located farther away.

Is the sink in the most useful place? Traditionally, it is sited under the window for ease of plumbing and to give the sink user

Rustic style on a grand scale. This kitchen with built-in units manages to avoid a clinical look with the clever use of varied textures, natural woods, soft paintwork colors and lots of homey clutter. It is a family space and, as is clear from the impressive array of hanging cooking pans and utensils, it is used by an eager cook to produce wonderful meals.

an outside view. However, you may prefer to plumb in a dishwasher and put your table by the window. Would this mean an expensive re-plumbing job?

The large kitchen is one of the most difficult to plan. The temptation, if you can afford it, is to fit in yards of cabinets, but perhaps you do not really need so many. It may suit you very well to keep the working part of your kitchen small and contained at one end or corner of the room so that the rest of the space can be given over to a large table for family meals.

Another option is to build in an island unit. This acts as a sort of work station and can be the place for a large, uninterrupted work surface or perhaps burners and/or a second sink for preparation.

How do I want to use this space?

First of all, you should think carefully about your lifestyle and the sort of cooking you have time for and enjoy. If you have a demanding job that leaves limited time for cooking or entertaining, there is little to be gained by spending huge sums of money on an expensive built-in kitchen and truckloads of the latest stoves, food processors, and a host of other gadgets. Your efforts will probably be best spent smartening up the room with a coat of fresh paint, a good quality fridge-freezer to store prepared foods, and a microwave.

For those who like informal meals shared with family and friends,

finding room for a table should be a priority. There are few evenings more enjoyable than those spent sitting around a candlelit table with congenial company. If space is limited, perhaps a couple of under-used cabinets can be sacrificed to make more room for your table.

If, however, you like to entertain on a grand scale, you may prefer to keep guests at bay in another room. Unless you are extremely relaxed, having friends rifling through drawers to find the bottle opener can be intensely annoying when you are putting the final touches to the hollandaise sauce! If you cook regularly, then you are likely to want plenty of room for fresh ingredients.

If you have young children, you will be faced with a completely different set of needs. No matter how large your home, the kitchen will act as a magnet for all sorts of activities. Children will want to help with the cooking, play games, and use the table for drawing, coloring, and homework. The essential here is a rugged, serviceable table. For your own peace of mind, forget about anything with a finely polished surface – there are sure to be spills and scratches and the odd slip of the pens and crayons. A good solid pine top that is easy to scrub clean will save a lot of heartache. Storage for toys and games is also worth considering. A simple chest or small cupboard should do the trick.

At this early stage it is also valuable to consider the needs of elderly or disabled friends and family members and to try to incorporate

them in your plans if you can; for example, ramps can replace steps and wide doorways will allow room for wheelchairs.

What do I like and dislike?

Here is the opportunity for some very satisfying list making. You might not be able to afford all the things you like at once, but by making a list, you should be able to identify the priorities. The secret of success here is not just to take a look at your present kitchen, but also to remember what you liked and disliked about your last kitchen, and those of others.

A good place to start is style. Do you prefer built-in kitchens to those furnished with freestanding furniture? It would be a great waste to rip out and throw away perfectly good cabinetry if you can achieve a facelift simply by painting or changing the doors. If you are aiming for a rustic look, then try plain pine; if you want something a little more bright and streamlined, there are plenty of smooth-finished laminated doors available in a huge choice of colors. It is also worth remembering that it is a fairly straightforward task to dismantle the collection of cabinets you may have inherited and shuffle them around to suit your needs.

Think of color schemes, too. If you have a dark kitchen, you might like to transform it into a light, white space, or you could play on the darkness and turn it into an intriguing cavern. Perhaps you have some favorite china, colored cooking pots, or collection of pitchers that you would like to build a color scheme around?

Once the storage areas are decided, you can think about countertops. Solid wood looks wonderful, but to prevent warping and splitting, it often needs maintenance. Stones such as marble and granite also look fabulous; they have the added benefit of needing little attention to keep them looking good, but they can be astronomically expensive. A slightly less expensive option here is terrazzo – a composite of stone fragments. Ceramic tiles are hardwearing and can look superb; however, they can look ugly if they are not laid properly and the grouting has a tendency to stain. One of the least expensive and toughest options is laminate. This is available in many colors and patterns and is extremely tough.

Next to consider are wall coverings and floorings. There is a huge choice available (see page 86). In the meantime, think carefully about your requirements; ceramic floor tiles may look great, but they can be cold to walk on – would vinyl be better?

Lighting can be extremely difficult to get right (see page 84). Ask yourself whether you like side lighting or a central fixture, working in bright light or a slightly muted glow?

Finally in this section, consider what sort of kitchen appliances you like to use. If you have the option, do you prefer cooking by gas or electricity? Do you like floor or wall-mounted ovens? Is a dishwasher a good idea?

What can I achieve within my budget?

Be absolutely realistic about what you can afford. Build in an emergency fund of ten percent for the unexpected. If you are planning to live with this kitchen for only a short time, do not be tempted to spend a fortune on it.

Finally, make yourself the promise that you will shop around and compare prices. Aim to get three quotations for any work, and never take the first you are offered.

The use of white gives a kitchen a clean, fresh look. The central, freestanding burners inset into a work surface make an unusual feature. The idea of adding a central island adds interest to the large room and provides a bench for informal eating and drinking.

Kitchen Planning and Design

There is no end of advice available on kitchen design; however, essentially, what we all want is a kitchen that functions well for our needs, that has adequate and convenient storage space, that is comfortable to work in, and of course, that looks good.

When starting your design, remember to refer to your notes on how you want to use the space and your likes and dislikes. It is important at this early stage to build in consideration for those who are very tall or very short and for kitchen users who may have disabilities and special needs. Kitchen manufacturers produce built-in units in standard sizes which are based on a module 24 inches wide x 24 inches deep x 36 inches high). While many variations of width and depth are available, few offer different height options. If you are very tall, one solution to the height problem is to raise the entire kitchen on blocks; if you are short, you could remove part of the base to lower the overall height. The disadvantage of tailoring your kitchen so specifically is that if you move, prospective buyers may take exception to your alterations.

To help you in your planning and design, we discuss here the five classic kitchen shapes and how to make the most of your available space.

The U-shaped kitchen

This is an extremely practical layout to work with as you are likely to have just one doorway interrupting your plan. If you choose built-in cabinets, this shape offers the opportunity for a continuous run of work surface around most of the room. Even the tiniest spaces perform well as everything will be within easy reach.

The classic layout for this type of kitchen is to place tall items such as an upright fridge-freezer at one end of the U and, at the other, a broom cupboard or wall-mounted oven. If you opt for this layout, and you have a door opening into the space, make sure there is adequate clearance for the door to swing open without crashing into you as you carry food in and out of refrigerator or oven. The ideal solution is to make the door outward-opening, fit a space-saving sliding door, or to remove the door altogether.

To make good use of all the space, and to slightly soften the room's angularity, you may want to set the stove or sink across the corner. Triangular-shaped sinks are designed for this purpose. In a narrow U-shaped room, make sure there is plenty of space to open fridge and oven doors without bumping into cabinets behind.

The L-shaped kitchen

If the room is very large, you may opt to arrange your units and appliances along just two walls to form an L-shaped work area. This design will cut the walking distance between sink, refrigerator, and stove, and should leave space for a table opposite.

This layout works well in both large and narrow rooms. As mentioned above, in a large room you will have space to fit cabinets and appliances along two walls and have room left for a table. If the space allows, you might even add a counter to one end of the L, to enclose the food preparation and cooking area and separate it from the eating area. The counter could also function as an eating bar.

The galley kitchen

This is the name usually applied to kitchens shoe-horned into a tiny

This handsome, freestanding storage unit serves many useful functions. It has plenty of room for displaying attractive dishes, and in the two end piers there is space to stow linen, candlesticks, and other dining items. The piece also acts as a room divider to screen off the dining area.

space with a door or opening at each end. This passage-like arrangement has the disadvantage of being walk through; however, good planning will make the best use of your space. An efficient layout plan places the sink and stove on one side of the room, preferably with natural light, with the refrigerator opposite.

The line kitchen

There are many line kitchen arrangements, ranging from those in large kitchen/dining rooms to others in a wide corridor.

The line arrangement enforces great design discipline. Keep the central section or work surface as uninterrupted as possible. A completely workable plan is to start with a small area of work surface, followed by stove, then the longest stretch of surface, completed by the sink and draining board. The fridge can be placed anywhere in the line.

The island kitchen

This really only works when you have the luxury of plenty of floor area. The island can consist of a block of storage units with a plain work surface, or the central block can incorporate burners and/or a sink. The size of your budget is important when considering the second option, as you will face the additional plumbing costs of running the services – water, electricity, and/or gas – through or beneath the floor. A central burner unit may also need an extractor fan.

Central islands also offer the option of two different work heights

recommended by the ergonomics experts; the regular height is good for general food preparation, and a slightly lower level is ideal for tasks such as pastry rolling and dough kneading which require more muscular effort.

The work triangle

When you start to draw a layout plan, you will come across the phrase "the work triangle." This is the design concept commonly used to make sure the kitchen is easy and comfortable to work in. It means that the sink, stove, and refrigerator will form the points of your triangle.

The key to success is to have an uninterrupted work area running between sink and stove. The ideal length is somewhere around one or two yards. Less than one yard and you will feel cramped; longer than two and you will be wasting time and energy moving around the space. The refrigerator position is the most flexible of the triangle. Ideally, for convenience, that too should be within a couple of yards of sink and oven.

The shape of your room and the position of windows and doors will, in part, dictate how you should plan your layout. Take time to stand back and consider all your options. Does the room have any intriguing architectural details that you can emphasize or enhance? Perhaps there is an interesting chimney nook that can be used to frame or display a small piece of sculpture or beautiful pitcher? Can the cornice be picked out in a color contrasting with the rest of the

The ultimate in sleek chic. This blonde wood built-in kitchen with its smooth surfaces and stainless steel handles and accessories is extremely neat. A single wall of cabinets contains all the electrical appliances you'd find in much larger rooms and with the built-in floor-to-ceiling units, there is a surprisingly generous amount of storage space.

room? Perhaps the style of window can be echoed in glass-fronted cabinets? Any major structural work will, of course, add to your budget. However, even fairly inexpensive alterations can pay huge dividends in making your kitchen an easier or pleasanter place in which to work. It is worth seeking professional advice and asking for a few quotes to discover how much or little you may need to spend.

Decide on the sink and stove positions first. The old school of design always placed the sink under the window – the thinking behind this was that you will spend a large proportion of your time standing at the sink and will want a view out. It also made – and, indeed, still makes – good sense to run plumbing along the outside wall. Today, however, we may prefer to make the most of the window's natural light by having it fall on a work surface or on a table. Dining at a table with a view can be infinitely preferable to dishwashing with a view.

Once you have selected the ideal position for the sink, try to place the stove nearby. If possible, allow for an area of work surface on both

sides of the burners, providing space for resting saucepans. The length of surface between sink and stove should be generous enough to provide plenty of space for food preparation and for stacking dirty dishes. Avoid locating an oven or stove near a doorway – it can be extremely dangerous.

As long as you do not place the refrigerator close to an inward-opening door, it can stand almost anywhere in the kitchen. If the refrigerator door has stationary hinges, make sure you can open it easily and safely.

Now that you have worked out your basic work triangle, you can start to plan the rest of your storage and work space.

Storage

Most people opt for a built-in kitchen to maximize the potential space for storage. However, the unfitted or non-kitchen look can make a welcome and refreshing alternative.

The design of the built-in kitchen has become very sophisticated, and the clever storage ideas are endless. Look out for devices such as sliding, pull-out pantrys, fold-away ironing boards, and corner cabinets with swivel racks.

In the unfitted kitchen, the pine dresser has traditionally provided the ideal space for storage and display, but for something a little more unusual, how about using a wooden armoire? Painted or plain wood, and fitted with shelves, an armoire is a great storage unit.

Bookcases and commercial display cabinets, too, can make excellent and practical storage spaces, which can be loaded with bottles, attractive jars, and cookbooks. With a little imagination, there is no limit to the types of furniture you can introduce to an unfitted kitchen – even an old office filing cabinet or chest of drawers can make the perfect place to store saucepans and baking sheets.

Shelving, as an alternative to built-in wall cabinets, gives the kitchen a lighter, more open feel. Shelves also provide an opportunity to create an attractive display with jars, bottles, glasses, or dishes. There are many types of shelving units and shelving kits available on the market, but if you want to try something unusual, consider using thick-gauge industrial glass, marble, concrete, bricks, or stainless steel. The freestanding stainless steel shelving units designed for professional kitchens can look extremely elegant loaded with stainless steel saucepans and kitchen equipment. Saucepans, large dishes, and cooking utensils may, alternatively, be stored on a trolley. Given a wooden or marble top, this could also double as a work surface.

Hanging rods and racks are becoming increasingly popular – especially for storing bulky items such as saucepans – and are ideal for small kitchens. Avoid any temptation to hang saucepans close to your stove as they will soon become greasy and dusty.

A number of manufacturers have produced wood and stainless steel

The unfitted kitchen has a great deal of charm. For an unfitted look, select pieces made of the same or similar material – in this case a rich, honey pine. The dresser has been a favourite item of kitchen furniture for centuries – it is extremely practical for storage and has plenty of space for displaying special items.

rods and racks, many of which are available with accessories such as clip-on trays for holding rolls of kitchen paper. A less expensive alternative is to mount a length of metal tubing, a wooden broom handle, or a towel rod to your kitchen wall (see page 92). Wall-hung plate racks are excellent, too, and allow you to keep everyday dishes within easy reach. When placed above the sink, they can double as a drainer.

In any kitchen, whether built-in or not, it is possible to work out a logical sequence of storage. Essentially, those things used most often should be stored close at hand, with the rule that the less frequently an item is used, the more distant it can be. It is wise to try to make sure that all objects are fairly easily accessible. A tightly packed cupboard is extremely uninviting, and the prospect of sorting through looking for a well-buried plate is so daunting that it will probably stay there forever, gathering dust.

Classic storage plans place garbage cans and cleaning materials under the sink. An alternative storage

such as saucepans, casserole dishes, food processors, and so on, should be stored in base cabinets. Placed high up they become difficult to lift up and down and could cause injury if they fall. If you have a dining table in the kitchen, it is a good idea to store dishes, flatware, and glasses in the nearest cabinet or shelf unit. A one-drawer unit is always useful for flatware, table linen, and small items of kitchen equipment.

Finishes for cabinets and countertops

The finishes you choose will set the style of your kitchen. As a guide, if you want to create a warm, comfortable feel, then choose from a palette of natural materials, particularly woods. For an efficient, hygienic style of kitchen, select smooth-finish laminates; for a clinical, uncluttered professional look, buy stainless steel.

To transform old kitchen cabinets you could simply add new decorative panels to the old doors and give them a coat of paint (see page 90). Or you could add new doors to the old cabinets. As long as your cabinets are sound and of a standard size, this can save a great deal of unnecessary expense and wasted materials in buying entirely new units. You can even achieve a bit of a facelift simply by replacing old handles.

Think carefully about your color choice. Dark shades, such as plum, bottle green, and navy blue, will look cozy and inviting, while pale tones will reflect more light and open out the room.

place for cleaning materials is a tall cabinet where you can also store a broom and ironing board. Cabinets and shelves above the sink should be used for light and small items

that are used regularly, such as cups, glasses, measuring cups, tea and coffee pots, everyday dishes, and dried, canned and bottled foods. Heavy and more bulky items,

Texture is extremely important, too. Unit doors with panels, wood and stone, and terracotta textures make a charming, rustic-style room; while smooth laminates and steel and ceramic look distinctly urban and chic.

Countertops are available in dozens of materials, textures, and patterns. One of the most popular, practical, and least expensive is laminate. This man-made material copes well with wear and tear, as it is tough, waterproof, hygienic, and scratch- and heat-resistant.

More expensive man-made materials include Corian, a type of artificial stone. Like laminate, it is hardwearing, easily wiped clean, and water and heat resistant. Unlike laminate, it is a solid material that can be cut and shaped to provide a smooth and seamless surface.

Woods, such as beech and maple, have an enduring appeal and are easily cut to the required size and shape. When oiled or varnished they are water resistant, but require occasional maintenance to keep them looking good. If well cared for, wood can improve with age. Always check the source of the wood you are buying – imported hardwoods may have been cut from rain forests or other unsustainable sources. Reputable suppliers will always be able to tell you where the wood has been grown.

Ceramic tiles are relatively inexpensive and hardwearing. However, they are prone to cracking and suffer from the problem of grubby grout. Water-resistant grout is available, but it may stain. When staining is severe, it is best to dig out old grout and replace it with new.

Stainless steel is the choice of the professional chef. It is durable, hygienic, easily cleaned, and heat and stain resistant. It will scratch, but this gives the material a charming patina.

Stones such as marble, granite and slate are heat- and stain-resistant and, although they can sometimes chip, they are generally very hardwearing. However, on the down side, they are also extremely expensive.

Safety and comfort tips

The kitchen is potentially the most dangerous place in the home. It is all too easy to cut, scald or bruise yourself, so bear in mind the following safety issues when making your plans:

• Make sure inward-opening doors do not crash into you while you are working. You could change the hinges to make the door open outward, install a sliding door, or remove it altogether.

• Do not hang anything flammable, such as curtains, dried flowers, or wooden spoons, near a naked flame. This warning applies to pilot lights as well as gas burners.

• Make sure that your kitchen is well ventilated. Gas appliances must have adequate ventilation.

• If you choose to hang a drying rack or saucepan rail from the ceiling, make sure there is plenty of headroom underneath. Make sure there is enough to spare even the tallest of guests from knocking themselves out on your favorite copper saucepan.

• Avoid storing heavy items, such as large cooking pans, pitchers, vases, bowls, or food processors, at the top of cabinets. They will be difficult and dangerous to remove.

• Always try and plan for a generous area of heatproof work surface at the side of stove where you can put saucepans and pots safely when removed from the heat.

• Install plenty of electric sockets in your kitchen. This reduces the opportunity of trailing dangerous cords across work surfaces.

• Never trail electrical cable across a cooker hob or sink.

• Consider finishing a run of units with a rounded end unit. This is a particularly good idea in a small kitchen as it will prevent you from bumping into sharp corners.

• Invest in a fire blanket and fire extinguisher.

• Leave a margin for error in units that must house appliances such as a washing machine or dishwasher. They are incredibly heavy and can be difficult to remove for repair if they fit too tightly.

• If you have young children, put a guard rail on your stove to stop them from reaching saucepans.

Wall coverings

Ceramic tiles: One of the most popular kitchen wall finishes, these are available in a huge variety of colors and patterns, are easy to install, relatively inexpensive, and offer a durable, stain-resistant, bright, easy-to-clean surface. The main drawback with ceramic tiles is that the grout tends to become grubby and stained. It can be scrubbed to remove the worst of the gathered dirt, but if stains persist, it is advisable to scrape out old grout and replace it with new. If tiles are placed in areas likely to be exposed to great heat, condensation, oil, or water splashes, make sure you install them with a water-resistant grout.

Tiles most usually appear in a horizontal band, two or three tiles deep, behind the work surface where they act as a splashback and as protection from dents and scratches (see page 88). They can also look stunning mounted on the entire height of the wall to ceiling level. Mosaics, many of which are sold in ready-assembled panels, are unusual and stylish.

Paint and paint effects: The most versatile of all finishes, paint

Kitchen color

Since most of your kitchen wall space will be taken up with cabinets and appliances, there may only be a small area of wall left to decorate. However, by paying careful attention to the detail, you will be able make the most of the overall look of your kitchen.

Green tiles and white kitchen cabinets combine to make a fresh and crisp kitchen color scheme. The effect is heightened with accessories in stainless steel, while the dazzling brightness is brought down to earth by the wood floor. A pale floor covering could have made the room feel unwelcoming.

is often all that is needed to transform a kitchen from a dowdy, depressing place to a welcoming one. In areas that require regular cleaning, such as behind a stove, or that are exposed to water splashes, such as behind a sink, oil-based mixtures are often the best choice. They will withstand more wear and tear and wiping and washing than water-based products.

Many manufacturers concerned about environment-damaging ingredients have now formulated eco-friendly blends. These solvent-free paints incorporate natural raw materials such as linseed oil, pine resin, chalk, and essential oils. They are pleasant to use and are particularly recommended for asthma and allergy sufferers.

If you are feeling adventurous, you could try a mural or any one of the many paint effects that are easily accomplished. Rag-rolling, sponging, and dragging have become rather over-used; however, stippling is a delicate and intriguing finish – special stippling brushes can be bought from most good paint stores. Among the most popular of paint decoration effects is stenciling. There are numerous specialist companies producing a vast array of stencil designs, complete with full instructions.

Wallpaper: This generally only works well in large kitchens with a separate dining area. In a small kitchen, hanging wallpaper behind and around cabinets can be a complete nightmare. You will also find that, unless you splurge on an expensive vinyl paper, the finish will not withstand the wear and tear of a busy kitchen and will soon become scruffy. However, if you do have the luxury of space for a dining area, wallpaper could provide the perfect solution to marking it off from the practical cooking area.

Wood: Many hardware stores now stock wood-paneling kits. You can opt for square panels or a tongue-and-groove style. This sort of finish works well when mounted from floor to work surface height to give you a half-paneled room. The wood is usually sold unfinished so you can varnish or paint it.

Stainless steel: Not frequently seen in home kitchens, stainless steel makes an ideal splashback behind work surfaces, stoves, and sinks. It is easy to install, inexpensive, extremely durable, easy to clean, stylish, and can be used to disguise uneven or damaged walls.

Plexiglas: If you are not fond of ceramic tiles, this tough, hygienic sheet material makes an ideal splashback. It is available in a wide choice of colors but, in its clear form, it can be mounted over a painted wall so you still see the paint color, with added protection against knocks and splashes in the most vulnerable areas – behind the burners and above the sink.

Color schemes

By the time you come to decorate your walls, you will certainly have thought long and hard about color schemes. You will have made some decisions already by choosing the units and furniture for the space. Even if you have chosen a minimalist white or stainless steel finish for the room you will still need to inject a bit of color to make it look more interesting. You could use brightly colored pans as a contrast, cheerful ceramics or a beautiful picture or photograph. Personal preference and association are powerful ingredients in making your choice. A very good idea is to build a scheme around a collection of china, a favorite painting or poster, or a theme such as the country kitchen or the Mediterranean kitchen.

In practical terms, you should take into account the colors of the cabinets and furniture already chosen. Blues, yellows, and white look wonderful with wood finishes, a pewter color looks chic with stainless steel, garlic pink looks great with wood and steel, and so on. Also take note of the amount, quality, and timing of natural light that floods the room. North-facing rooms receive little or no direct sunlight, east windows receive the weak morning sun, west-facing rooms get the rich evening light, and south-facing will receive direct sunlight through most of the day. To warm up the feel of a room, choose from the red end of the spectrum; to produce a cooling effect, use blues and greens.

It is interesting to note that colors can have a strong psychological and even physical effect on us. Reds have been shown to quicken the heartbeat, increase blood pressure, and stimulate taste buds (the reason why restaurants are decorated using red); blues have the opposite effect. Virulent lime greens can make people feel uncomfortable (in experiments, when used in company washrooms, lime green walls dramatically reduced the time people spent there), and pinks can be calming (pink shades have been used in prison cells to quieten aggressive prisoners).

As a general rule when choosing paint, light colors will open out a space and dark will close it in. Turn attractive doors and window frames into features. Picking out woodwork in a color that is darker than the walls will draw attention to those details and give it emphasis.

A badly lit room may look at its best simply decorated in white. White does, in fact, suit almost every kitchen because of its associations with cleanliness and purity. Breaking the rules can produce successful results, too – for example, a rich navy blue or emerald green, or the two together, can look fabulous in tiny spaces and gives the effect of a glittering jewel box.

The classic combination of red and green is shown to dramatic effect in this light and spacious kitchen. The darkness of the cabinets is offset by the pale wallpaper, the stripped door, and wood table. Red and green accessories continue the theme.

Kitchen appliances

If you are planning to spend seriously large amounts of money on your kitchen, you will have no problem at all finding expensive, deluxe, multi-functional, super-efficient appliances sporting control panels bristling with so many buttons, dials and displays they would look completely at home in the cockpit of a jumbo jet. However, back down on earth, the rest of us are more likely to be looking for good quality, efficiency, and value for money. Whatever the size of your budget, there is plenty of choice.

Of growing concern in this area is the production of machines that are environment-friendly. Many have been designed and developed to maximize efficiency and use less water, less detergent, and less energy than previous models. Many kitchen appliance manufacturers have taken the green message extremely seriously and now package their goods in environment-friendly, recycled and recyclable materials, finish them with low-solvent or solvent-free paints, and design machines in such a way that makes it possible to recycle components easily at the end of the appliance's useful life.

Burners, ovens and microwaves

The first consideration when buying any sort of cooking appliance is the fuel you intend to use. Electricity and gas are clean, efficient, and available just about everywhere, although it is worth noting that a natural gas supply can be difficult to come by in rural areas. If you have access to both the main fuels, the most effective cooking combination is gas burners, ideal for instant heat and precise control, and an electric oven. Fan ovens are the most energy efficient as they circulate hot air continuously to cook faster. Decide just how much and what style of cooking you are likely to undertake. For example, if you are

not very interested in cooking and prefer convenience or prepared meals, then a microwave oven and a standard, no-frills oven will be all you need. If, however, you have the time for, and interest in, more traditional methods of cooking, you will opt for a built-in stove. For the real enthusiast, there is also the option of a freestanding professional-style stove. While these are a joy to cook with, they are extremely expensive. In tiny kitchens, where space is at a premium, compact ovens and double burners are now available.

The styles of stoves and ovens include freestanding units incorporating oven, burners, and perhaps also a separate broiler, and, with the same sort of functions,

slide-in machines designed to slot into a space between built-in units. This is a considerably less expensive option than installing separate oven and burners. In addition, there are many styles of built-in appliances: single and double ovens that fit under counters and others, perhaps combining a large and small oven or microwave and broiler, designed to fit in a tall cabinet that stretches between floor and ceiling. This latter design is an expensive option because of the cost of the housing unit, but is excellent for those with back problems or physical disabilities as it eliminates the need for bending down to remove hot dishes from the oven. If your kitchen is being designed with the elderly or disabled in mind, always make sure that controls on appliances are easy to turn on and off and are clear and easy to read. For safety, especially if there are young children around, it is important to check that oven doors are well insulated and remain cool when they are in use.

Other considerations include the fact that ovens with an integral broiler can be annoying, as you will not be able to bake and broil at the same time. In addition, the broiler elements can become spotted with grease from baking and smoke very badly when first switched on. Take

For the really serious cook, there are few appliances to beat the Aga-style stove. The French machine pictured here features two electric ovens, four gas burners and a large gas-fired griddle. This is virtually a professional standard appliance.

note of the way an oven door opens, with a left, right, or bottom hinge? The left- and right-hinged types require less opening space, which may be more convenient for small kitchens.

If you are installing a separate oven and burners, your choice of burner will depend on the type of cooking fuel you use and your budget. With built-in kitchens, there is no necessity to have burners and oven close to each other. You may find it convenient, for example, to fit the burners into the same work surface as the sink and choose to place the oven in a wall unit elsewhere in the kitchen.

The most modern and expensive burners are the smooth-surfaced ceramic variety; they glow when hot and are easily wiped clean. Among the latest cooking innovations are touch-sensitive controls and electric halogen light elements – these allow you to cook using light which heats up and cools down in seconds.

The microwave oven, with its ability to defrost, heat and cook foods, has found favor in countless kitchens. Many people find them invaluable for cooking prepared or frozen meals at the end of a busy day. Sophisticated versions of the microwave are described as combination ovens. These incorporate a broiler and fan to brown foods and cook them in a conventional way. The machines have the advantage of being quick to use, economical to run, easy to accommodate even in the smallest of kitchens, and easy to clean.

Exhaust fans

The favorite choice of exhaust is the type that is installed above the stove and enclosed in a hood. You will be offered the choice between those that draw the air away from the cooking area and expel it outside and others that take air through a filter and re-circulate it in the room. The first is usually the most efficient and works best when stove and hood are fitted on an outside wall, keeping the distance of ducting to a minimum.

One of the most common complaints voiced about exhaust fans is the whirring noise they make. This problem can sometimes be solved quickly and simply by replacing or cleaning the filter, which may have become clogged by grease. Another, more expensive solution is to fit a larger or more powerful exhaust. Check the manufacturer's instructions to see what capacity is recommended for the size of your kitchen.

Refrigerators and freezers

Once again, your lifestyle and level of interest in cooking will dictate what sort of refrigerator and/or freezer you buy. If there are just two of you in the home and you do not cook often, a refrigerator to fit under a work surface with an integral freezer compartment may be all you need. Those who cook frequently will need a large refrigerator for storing fresh produce – large salad drawers are essential. If you use a lot of convenience and frozen foods, you will need a larger freezer section

and may opt for an upright unit which is half refrigerator, half freezer. Horizontal fridge-freezers are also very useful as they can slot under a work surface.

Unless you have a large family, beware of buying a large freezer. You could find that you are storing goods unnecessarily, and at considerable expense, for months and even years. Very small and slim-line refrigerators and freezers are available for tiny kitchens.

Before buying your refrigerator or freezer, check which way its doors open. If they are wrong for you, ask if they can be changed – many appliances now offer this option. You may also want a unit that allows you to mount a decor panel on the door to match the other doors in a built-in kitchen.

Dishwashers

Great strides have been made in improving the performance, energy, water and detergent consumption of dishwashers since they first arrived on the scene. Indeed, many are now so efficient that manufacturers claim they can save at least forty per cent of the cost of washing dishes by hand.

The best designs incorporate good insulation, allowing them to operate much more quietly than ever before. Noise and vibration can be reduced even more by setting the appliance on a rubber mat. They should also include an antiflood device, easy sliding trays, and good filtration to keep clean water in circulation.

Corners are often considered dead space and places where unnecessary clutter can accumulate. However, imaginative planning and design have made good use of the corner space in this kitchen as the site for the stove and exhaust fan hood.

Washing machines

Machines are designed either as top-loading or front-loading – the latter is ideal for slotting under a kitchen work surface. They are also sold in styles that will allow you to mount a decor panel to match the rest of your kitchen cabinets. Unless you have access to, or like to use, outdoor space for drying, it is best to buy an integrated washer-dryer. If you have plenty of space in your kitchen area, a separate washing machine and tumble dryer can be considered. These can stand side by side or one on top of the other.

Sinks and waste disposal

The humble kitchen sink is no longer so humble. There is now the option to use it with accessories such as an integrated chopping board, waste chute, colander basket, vegetable and salad washer, plate rack, and retractable spray. If you are a keen cook, buy the largest sink possible. In small kitchens, one-and a-half bowls plus drainer serves well and triangular, corner-fitting sinks make good use of awkward space. Before buying any sink, make sure it will be compatible with your built-in cabinets; very deep models may not be suitable for some systems.

It is a good idea to decide at the kitchen planning stage whether or not you would like and can afford a waste disposal unit, as it is easiest to install them alongside the rest of the plumbing work. Some manufacturers also offer waste chutes to dispose of compost-type waste matter, such as fruit and vegetable trimmings, through a neat trap in the work surface.

Sinks are now offered in a variety of materials. The stainless steel and ceramic types have become very popular for traditional-style kitchens. There are also several varieties of plastics; although the

ones with textured finishes have a tendency to stain. New on the scene are the stone and resin composite sinks. These look extremely elegant, with a speckled finish that is very durable.

Few materials have surpassed stainless steel, which is pressed from a sheet and so has no seams in which germs and dirt can be harbored. It also wears extremely well. Stainless steel comes in a variety of thicknesses; buy the thickest gauge possible.

Before buying faucets, make sure they are compatible with your sink.

Kitchen lighting

Lighting can make or break a room. It can also create or ruin a mood. Glaring lights will literally put you in the spotlight and will generate a feeling of unease. Inadequate lighting will cast a shadow of gloom over the room, making it unwelcoming and dowdy. The perfect balance is achieved by installing general room lighting, either ceiling or wall-hung, and good, crisp lighting over work areas (this is called task lighting).

The lighting you choose should be sympathetic to the kitchen decor and the ways in which you use the room. A pine-based kitchen will look cozy and homey with table lamps, while a modern-style, windowless galley kitchen is likely to need sparkly, low-voltage halogen fixtures.

Working with electricity involves a great deal of potential danger and installing new lights is a skilled job. Unless you are entirely competent, it is highly recommended that you employ an expert. Always check fixtures for the recommended maximum bulb wattage – if this is exceeded, you may damage the lamp.

Types of lighting

Tungsten: This is the light provided by regular household bulbs. The clear bulb will cast a warm, slightly yellow light. In addition, there are many pearl-finished and colored bulbs now on the market. Tungsten strips are also sold.

Fluorescent: This is most commonly used as strip lighting. Fluorescent tubes are available in a wide variety of lengths; they are long-lasting and energy-efficient and therefore cheap to run. Due to its blue-white color, fluorescent is rather harsh lighting and should ideally be mounted behind a shield, perhaps under a cabinet, to shine light on the work surfaces.

Halogen: The low-voltage halogen light has become increasingly popular because it emits a sparkling white light. The drawbacks are that lights must be fitted with transformers and that the bulbs themselves, while long-lasting if treated with care, are fragile and expensive.

Designing your lighting scheme

When you start to design your kitchen lighting scheme, bear in mind both practical and esthetic considerations. The first is to make sure you have adequate and practical light in which to work safely; to avoid shadows, make sure the light is cast directly on your countertop and not on you. The second is related to "painting" your space with light; you may wish to highlight certain areas and play others down.

Most rooms have a central, ceiling-suspended fixture that takes a tungsten bulb. This is a start, but, even with an attractive shade, the effect is often stark and utilitarian in feel. Overhead lighting also casts shadows and has a tendency to give the effect of lowering ceiling heights. Depending on your taste, a central overhead light can be supplemented by wall-mounted lights (these should be placed above eye-level to give a gentle, inviting glow), or perhaps a couple of ever-versatile table lamps. Dimmer switches are more expensive than regular controls, but they are an extremely good investment as they allow great flexibility. Other options include converting your central overhead light into a rise-and-fall lamp that can be brought down to illuminate a dining table, work surface or counter, and then lifted out of the way again when not required.

Alternatively, track lighting could be installed with several spotlights which can be angled to wherever they are most needed. Recessed lighting is also effective and flexible. These fixtures are set into the ceiling and can be positioned directly over work surfaces or, if they are the sort with a movable "eyeball" center, can be used as wall washers or to highlight specific objects or areas. Recessed lamps are particularly useful in rooms with low ceilings – you will not need to duck under the bulbs.

If you have a high ceiling, an excellent way of throwing light up is to mount small uplighters above wall-hung cabinets or on high shelves. Light will bounce off the ceiling and fall as a soft glow.

The secret of using fluorescents effectively is to conceal the tubes behind the baffle at the bottom of wall cabinets. The baffle shields your eyes from direct glare, and the light is cast directly onto the work surface without creating annoying, and dangerous, shadows that may interfere with your food preparation. It is essential to have this sort of unobstructed task lighting to allow you to see clearly as you work. Before you install your lighting, you should also check that the baffle protects you from glare at your table.

Halogen lighting is now available in a number of styles: in small tracks sprouting a number of bulbs, recessed, or in single lamps. The bulbs are sold as spots, which cast a pool of concentrated light, or wide angle, which shed larger pools with softer edges. Installing halogen is a specialist task as it requires transformers.

These are sold as small, heavy boxes or cigar-shaped tubes which transform the powerful voltage into a low-voltage supply. Transformers can be set either close to the light source or remotely. They usually emit a slight hum and so are best placed inside the ceiling recess or,

perhaps, a cabinet. While manufacturers are making progress with this new technology, dimmer switches, as yet, rarely work successfully with low-voltage halogen. They can emit an annoying and ear-piercing whine.

Last, but by no means least, there are candles. For obvious practical and safety reasons, these are not recommended for everyday lighting. However, for special occasions and romantic suppers, candlelight is difficult to beat.

In this small kitchen the lack of natural light is counteracted by the use of stainless steel, which reflects the artificial light and bounces it around the room.

Kitchen flooring

Beautiful flooring really does make a huge difference to a room, and you do not need to spend a fortune to achieve excellent results. Of course, if your budget is unlimited, you might like to lay stone or slate, but the chances are that you will have to be more realistic. Even where the purse is bottomless, you may not be able to fit some types of finishes, such as flagstones, or ceramic and terracotta tiles, if your floor cannot take the weight.

If you do have a solid floor on which to work, then the choices of finish are many and varied: limestone, granite, ceramic tiles, terracotta, wood, vinyl, cork, or linoleum. The options open to those with wooden floors are the lighter materials.

Your choice of color and pattern is also important. A plain-color floor, especially if it is white, will show every mark. Some small fleck or pattern will spare you hours of cleaning. That said, floors with a light-colored base will brighten a room, while darker shades will close it in. Lively patterns can overwhelm a kitchen. A large room can look stunning with a bold black and white checkerboard design, but this treatment could completely swamp a small room. In smaller spaces, a plain finish is infinitely preferable. If in doubt, keep it simple.

Types of flooring

Wood: If you are lucky enough to have good floorboards (most are hardwearing pine), this provides a wonderful opportunity to achieve a stripped and varnished finish at a reasonable cost. The advantages of wood are that it is durable, chic, warm, and can improve with age. The disadvantages are that it can dent and scar if damaged by heavy or sharp objects, it is not particularly good at providing soundproofing, and it will need some maintenance from time to time and occasional re-varnishing.

Cleaning old floorboards is backbreaking and dusty work, but the finished result is well worth the effort. You will probably need to replace some of the damaged boards and rent a professional sanding machine to lift off the worn and grubby top surface. If new boards are a lighter color than your existing ones, you can "age" them by painting on a couple of coats of cold, black tea. Once you have achieved an even surface and cleared away all the dust, paint the boards with several coats of tough varnish for a rich, glowing, warm and hardwearing finish. For a pickled effect, paint the sanded boards with watered-down white latex and then protect with flat varnish.

An easier alternative for a good-quality wood finish is possible with the veneer and laminate packs available from hardware stores. The laminate finish is virtually indestructible. It resists damage from grit and sharp heels, stains, and cigarette burns. These packs are sold in a variety of styles and colors, from prepared wood "tiles" composed of small wooden strips mounted on a backing material, to lengths of tongue-and groove. The tiles will give the effect of a parquet or wood block floor, while the tongue-and-groove system resembles neat boards. These packs are sold either ready varnished or untreated so that you can stain and varnish them yourself.

Vinyl: This incredibly tough material is stain resistant, waterproof, easy to wash and clean, and warm to the touch. It is available in a wide choice of thicknesses and prices, in sheets or tiles. As a general rule of thumb, the thicker it is, the more it costs.

To achieve the best results with this material, it is essential to start with a well-prepared, flat base. Blackboard or masonite are ideal. Using a recommended adhesive, both tiles and sheets are easy to lay and are virtually maintenance free.

Linoleum: This finish shares many of the properties of vinyl. It is warm, stain resistant, durable, easily washable, and is also available in sheet or tile form. In recent years, linoleum has enjoyed a revival of popularity because it is manufactured using natural materials. As demand has increased, so has the choice.

Cork tiles: Easy to clean, warm underfoot, inexpensive, tough, easy to lay, and with an intriguing, mottled finish, cork has remained popular for years. As with wood and vinyl, the answer to a perfect finish with cork tiles lies in meticulous preparation and a flat base. Spread the recommended adhesive over the entire surface of the tile to make sure you achieve a good, firm bond.

Tiles are sold prepared with a vinyl coating or in their natural state. Sealing is essential to provide water resistance and durability.

Ceramic tiles: Ceramic tiles are hardwearing, easily cleaned, and available in all price ranges; not surprisingly, the best quality tiles are the most expensive. Their disadvantages are that they are hard, cold underfoot, noisy, and often slippery when wet. Almost without exception, they should be laid on solid floors. For the best results, tiles should be laid professionally.

Terracotta tiles: Terracotta (baked clay) has a warm, red-brick color that becomes wonderfully soft and muted with age. Because these tiles are heavy, they are best laid on solid floors.

Stone, slate, and marble: For those with solid floors and a large budget, these finishes can look fabulous. All are extremely

hardwearing and expensive. They are also hard, cold, and tend to be noisy. They are difficult to cut and lay, so this work should be carried out by professionals.

Terrazzo: An aggregate composed of stone and glass chips and concrete, this gives a tough, colorful finish. It is available in tiles or slabs and is best laid on solid floors because of its heavy weight. Once again, it is worth paying an expert to lay this sort of flooring.

The rustic style of open wooden beams, the heavy stone fireplace, and pine furniture is complemented by the sturdy red brick flooring. This sort of porous material is difficult to keep spotlessly clean, but does collect a wonderful patina with age.

Project 11

Tiling the wall behind your work surface

Tiling a small area like this is possible even for the least experienced at do-it-yourself – and, with a little patience and care, the results will look excellent.

The key to success is good preparation. Before starting work, make sure you have all the materials and tools on hand and the time necessary to complete the job.

Measure the space to be tiled to estimate the number of tiles you will need. It is always a good idea to buy a few spares just in case you break a couple while installing them, or in case of later damage when you may need replacements.

When buying the adhesive and grout, read the instructions carefully to make sure you have the right type and the correct quantity. If in doubt, ask; all good hardware shops will be able to offer advice.

Tools and Materials

- two wood battens, ⅓ x ½ inch and long enough to frame one side and the length of area to be tiled
- Carpenter's level
- small nails or brads
- adhesive (make sure the pack includes a spreader)
- tiles (as estimated, plus a few spare ones)
- pack of tile spacers
- tile cutter
- water-resistant grout

1 Make sure the area of wall to be tiled is sound and smooth. Remove all traces of old wallpaper or old tiles, chip off any loose paint or wall plaster. If necessary, fill cracks and holes with a plaster putty and smooth with sandpaper.

2 Using a pencil and the wood battens, mark out area to be tiled. Draw a grid of tile positions on the wall, leaving grouting space of about ⅛ inch between each tile. An important consideration here is that the top row is composed of whole tiles; cut tiles along the top will look messy. Use the level to make sure the lines are even. Using small nails or brads, fix one of the battens along the lowest horizontal line. The tiling between this batten and the work surface will be completed at the end of the job. It is also a good idea to put up a vertical batten to keep the lines straight. Both battens will be removed when the job is complete.

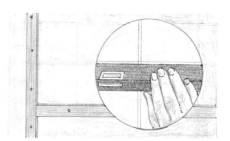

3 Most tile adhesive is sold with a spreader (a flat piece of plastic with one notched edge) inside the pack. Use this tool to spread adhesive directly onto the wall - it usually needs to be about ⅛ inch deep, but check directions for recommended thickness. When you are tiling a large area, apply adhesive in sections of around 1 square yard at a time.

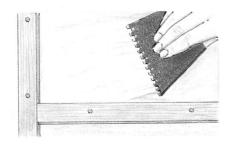

4 Lay the first tile at the right-angled corner made by the two battens. Press firmly into place. Continue along the horizontal line, using spacers between each tile. Check that the tiles in the first row have stuck well before starting on the line above. Continue until the whole area is tiled.

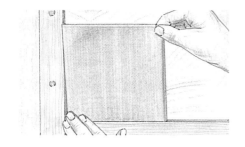

5 Let it dry for a day before filling tile gaps with grout. Make sure the grout is pressed firmly into the gaps and remove any excess with a damp cloth. Once the grout has dried, prize off the battens and fill any holes made by the nails. Finish the job by completing the last line of tiling and grouting.

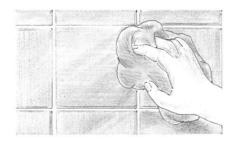

Project 12

Decorative panels for unit doors

There are many ways to give your kitchen a facelift and improve the look of old cabinets. Adding a coat of paint or stenciling on patterns are among the options, but you may also like to add decorative paneling. Paneling kits are now widely available in hardware stores, and they are inexpensive and easy to fit. Make sure that you measure the doors carefully before buying your kit.

If you cannot find the right kit, it is easy to make the panels for yourself from the moldings sold in lumberyards and hardware stores. To make these, you will need the length of the chosen molding, a saw, and a miter box - the box helps you to saw accurate corners. Measure the size of panel required, cut wood to length, then join with brads pins and glue for extra strength.

Before you begin, make sure the doors are clean and free from grease. Use liquid detergent or a little pure vinegar on stubborn grease marks.

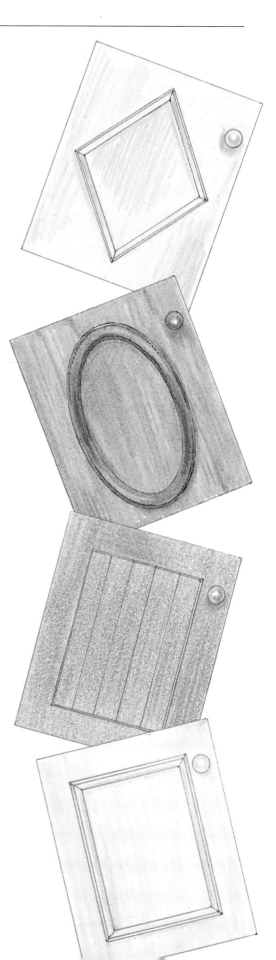

Tools and Materials

- paneling kit or the own homemade panels (see above)
- Carpenter's level
- adhesive (if not supplied in the kit)

1 Using a pencil, mark the position of the panels on the doors. Take great care to make sure the lines are even – use a level if you are unsure.

2 Hold the panels in place to make sure that they look right. The adhesive used in most kits is already applied to the underside of the panels; all you need to do is peel off the protective backing strip. If you are glueing on your own panels, draw a thin line on the back of the panels with wood glue.

3 With the adhesive exposed, place the panels against the door and maneuver into place. Press firmly to adhere. Leave to bond and dry.

Project 13

A saucepan rack

This is a useful way of storing bulky items like saucepans, while also keeping them within easy reach. A number of manufacturers produce a variety of racks, but it's also possible to make your own using a chrome or stainless steel clothesrod.

Select the most convenient area for the rack and check that the wall is in good condition and will have the strength to carry the weight of a number of saucepans. Walls constructed of brick or plaster are ideal. Thin wood or wallboard will not support the weight.

Tools and Materials

- 2 supports
- metal tubing cut to the required length
- electric or hand drill
- wall anchors
- screws
- metal butcher's hooks

 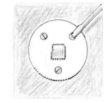

2 Drill the holes and push in anchors. Screw the first support into place. Slot in the rod, then mount the second support.

3 Rest butcher's hooks on the rod and hang the saucepans.

1 Hold up the rod and supports and, with a pencil, mark the places where you will need to drill holes. Remove the rod and supports.

Project 14

Storing recyclable materials

With the growing interest in recycling household waste material comes the need to store it neatly. If your aim is to be environment-friendly, it is a good idea to start with your own environment and keep that clean and neat.

This rack is designed to take three kinds waste material: glass, newspapers, and cans. It can stand on its end while it is being filled and then turned up to form a carrying crate to dispose of the waste.

Tools and Materials

- saw
- 8 x 14⅜ inch lengths of ¾ x ¾ inch wood
- 8 x 12 inch lengths of 1¾ x ½ inch wood
- 8 x 22¾ inch lengths of 1¾ x ½ inch wood
- 1 piece ¼ inch plywood, 22¾ x 1¾ inch
- 2 pieces ¼ inch plywood, 14⅜ x 12 inches
- ¾ inch nails
- hammer
- wood glue

1 Take two lengths of ¾ x ¾ inch wood and, at equal distances, nail and glue on four 12-inch lengths of 1¾ x ½ inch wood. Repeat the exercise. This will make the top and bottom sections.

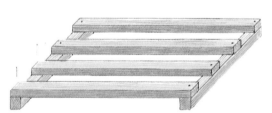

2 Take one of the sections and, at equal intervals, nail and glue onto the ¾ x ¾ inch wood and four 22¾ inch lengths of 1¾ x ½ inch wood. Repeat the exercise on the other section. You now have a top and side section and a bottom and side section.

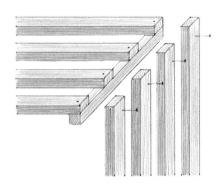

3 Nail and glue the two sections together. You now have the skeleton of the crate. When the glue is dry, nail and glue on the back panel of plywood.

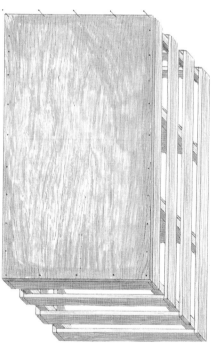

4 To make the shelves, nail and glue the four remaining ¾ x ¾ inch lengths of wood to the two side panels to form rests for the shelves. Let the glue set.

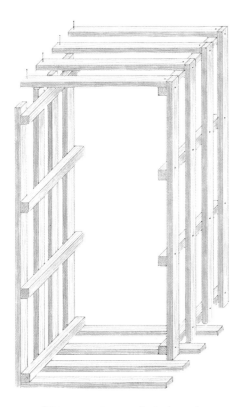

5 Slide the plywood shelves into place, glue, and nail.

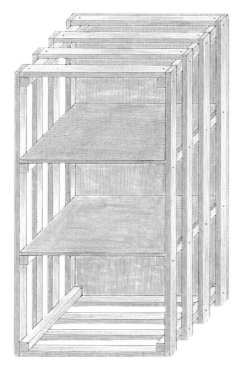

Project 15

New handles

Old or damaged handles can make doors and drawers difficult to open - and they look scruffy. New ones can give a kitchen a real lift. Select the new handles with care. Make sure they are in a finish that matches your decor; brass handles, for example, look odd next to stainless steel faucets, and very ornate Victorian handles will sit uncomfortably in a modern-style room.

Tools and Materials

- ruler
- yardstick
- required number of new handles
- suitable screws and hardware, if not supplied with handles
- screwdriver

1 Remove the old handles carefully, taking care not to cause damage. It may be that the new handles are of a completely different type from the existing ones, in which case you will need to fill the old holes with an appropriate putty and very carefully drill new ones.

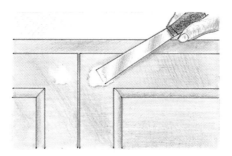

2 Take great care in measuring for new holes; if handles are out of alignment on a drawer unit, they will look very messy. Use a pencil to mark clearly where the handles are to be positioned and, using a yardstick, make sure they line up perfectly.

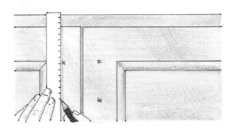

3 Fix new handles according to the manufacturer's instructions.

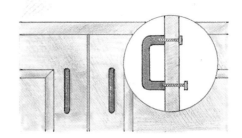

Chapter four

Your dining area

When it comes to decorating a dining room, the scheme will depend on several factors, such as whether it is a separate room or part of another, the existing furniture, the available light, and the mood you are trying to create. Your choice of color or theme could be inspired by your china or curtains – or maybe you need a neutral backdrop for stronger accent colors or interesting furniture. Red is a traditional color for dining rooms, and it does promote an intimate atmosphere for dinner parties, but it can be difficult to live with all the time and is best reserved for separate dining rooms. Whatever color combination or theme you choose, try to stick to it as closely as possible – too many different styles and colors can create a cluttered look and will feel claustrophobic. The type of furniture you choose will affect the style of the room – mahogany for a traditional look, light wood or wicker for a lighter, less formal look.

Seating

It is difficult to estimate how many people you can seat around a table. For a start, it depends on how friendly they want to get, but as a rule 24 inches per person is a good guide. If your chairs have arms, about the width of a pair of crossed arms – or 28 inches by a depth of 14 inches – is adequate for each place setting. Something else to bear in mind when seating people is the position of the table legs. Most of us have spent at least one uncomfortable meal with our legs straddling the table leg.

If you are trying to find chairs for a table you already own, take the height of the table with you when you go shopping. Chairs with arms should fit underneath the table for comfort and to save space. Try to allow 12 inches between the chair seat and the tabletop.

Table settings and room decoration

Decoration and furnishings are just a part of the finished look of your dining area. You can complete and change the overall effect with the type of table settings you create. Candles and flowers don't cost much, but they can really add a special touch. If you have time to make your own decorated fabric napkins, every meal will be an occasion.

Below left: Table settings don't have to be elaborate to be effective. If you find it difficult to arrange flowers, why not put a single stem in a vase?

Right: Give the dinner table a personal touch with some handmade napkins. Here, scraps of material have been used to make patchwork and appliqué designs, and a length of ribbon has been threaded through buttonholes for a really festive look.

Laying a table

Most dining is fairly casual these days, and when it comes to laying a table for dinner, there are no strict rules about how to do it.

Lay places so that guests are evenly spaced around the table, trying to give them a minimum of 24 inches each.

Place flatware according to the order of eating. The first pieces to be used should be on the outside of the setting, so that you start at the outside and work your way in. Knives (with the blade facing the plate) and spoons go on the right of each setting; forks on the left.

Glasses stand on the right above the knives and spoons. Use a wide

goblet for red wine or water, a small wine glass for white wine, and an even smaller version for sherry or liqueurs. If you are only using one glass, use a stemmed goblet.

The side plate (for bread or salad) should be on the left of the place setting and to the left of the flatware, with the napkin on top.

Special occasions

Decorating a table for dinner is the icing on the cake. Take time to plan what you are going to do and match it to the occasion.

Keep to a theme and follow it through to the china, flatware, napkins, and candles. Be creative: outline each place in trails of ivy; put a fresh flower on each plate; tie up silverware with ribbon; write the menu and place cards on handmade paper.

Your theme could be a birthday or a color to complement the room. Try painting glasses (see page 118) either to match china or with the name or favorite thing of a birthday celebrant. Use a length of plain cotton sheeting instead of a tablecloth and dye or paint it with

your own designs with fabric paints. It is cheap enough to use for one special occasion.

A centerpiece can be matched to the occasion. Keep it simple and effective: floating candles and flower heads in a bowl of water; flowers displayed in tin cans; an arrangement of candles of different heights; a pile of presents. Keep the centerpiece low so guests can talk to each other over it.

For a children's party, buy a pack of construction paper and use the sheets as table mats; cover the table with a paper tablecloth, give the children crayons, and let them draw; tie bright-colored balloons to the backs of chairs and let the guests take them home afterward.

Tablecloths and napkins

Unless you want it to be floor length, a tablecloth should have an all-round drop of 10–12 inches so that it falls a little below lap level and your guests don't get tangled up in it. To a certain degree, a cloth will protect the table, but a thick felt table pad underneath allows you to put warm plates and hot dishes safely on the cloth without damaging the table underneath.

Table felt is available from department stores, or look through the classified ads in home magazines for mail-order companies who will cut it to size to fit your table.

With so many pretty paper napkins available, it hardly seems worth bothering with the fabric variety. But fabric napkins do provide an opportunity to dress the table up and create a little theme on a plate. Be imaginative and use twisted ivy, ribbon, luggage tags, dried flower heads, raffia, beads, copper garden tags, and handwritten cards. Personalize each napkin for your guests.

For birthday meals, a little present attached to the napkin with ribbon is a nice touch; at Christmas, tie ornaments with curling ribbon; at Easter you could attach a little package of chocolate eggs tied up in pretty paper. There are loads of things you can do...

Fabric napkins don't need to be expensive. Cut them from remnants to match color schemes, or make each one different (see page 101). Scour the remnant boxes in shops for unusual fabrics at bargain prices. Dress fabrics are ideal for making napkins as they are designed to withstand regular washing. If you use upholstery fabrics, wash them first to remove any sizing or special finish.

Right: A napkin is a theme on a plate — ribbon, ivy, raffia, and luggage tags all make amusing and individual napkin rings.
Above left: At a children's party, sheets of paper make individual place mats to draw on, and the parcels decorating the table can be taken home as presents.

Multipurpose dining areas

Below: An impromptu dining area
can be set up in the corner of any room.
Right: Base cabinets separate
the kitchen and dining areas.

Most dining areas are borrowed from another room, usually the kitchen or living room, but a dining area in a large hall or conservatory is not unusual. New houses are often built with just one room downstairs that has to double as both the living and dining area. So how do you decorate a room that has to serve more than one purpose?

Create different moods by using lighting and furniture to highlight separate areas of the room while keeping the same color throughout.

Freestanding open shelves can divide a dining area from a living area without blocking any light and will provide useful storage space for both rooms. Two large rugs on a wooden floor can contain dining and living space within their boundaries.

Another way to create a separate dining area is by using a movable physical barrier such as a suspended screen to isolate a kitchen from its storage area (see page 106) or gauze on a curtain track (page 123). A freestanding screen will partially separate the table to give the dining area an intimate feel, and can be folded against the wall when not in use.

The space under the stairs is often under-used, yet this alcove can make a cozy dining area in a small house. Shelved, it will also provide valuable storage space for china and glassware. Another often-forgotten space for eating is the hall. Some older houses and apartments have enormous hallways that will easily accommodate a dining table and chairs. You may have to take a few extra draft-proofing measures, but such an arrangement could create a wonderfully welcoming entrance to any property.

Many people decide to build a sunroom to give themselves an extra room, and if there isn't a

separate dining room, this would be an ideal opportunity to create one. If you can, it is a good idea to choose a dining table and chairs specifically for the new room if you intend to use it for meals. Traditional dining furniture tends to be rather dark, so is probably not the best choice for a sunroom. Wicker chairs and tables are ideal and are often very reasonably priced. Add comfort and style with some leafy or flower print throw pillows, in keeping with the garden room theme. A glass table would be perfect because it would enhance the feeling of light and space. It makes the perfect setting for evening dinner parties, with the candlelight reflected in the glass.

Many modern homes and apartments have an open-plan kitchen at one end of the dining room. These can be turned to practical and decorative advantage. Install double-sided cabinets to separate the two areas – the ones on the kitchen side could store food, pans, and cooking utensils, while those next to the dining area would contain glasses, dishes, and flatware.

A dining room may also need to be an office, sewing room, den, or playroom, so you must think about how you will use the room before you decide what sort of furniture it will require.

A large dining table can double as a sewing table or, if the dining room is to be used as an office, you might prefer a smaller table to leave plenty of room for filing cabinets and a computer table. There may be a need for extra storage for hobbies, or for a small desk for studying or doing household accounts.

It could be that this is the only room in the house where it is possible to get any peace and quiet – perhaps an armchair and footstool would fit in, along with a shelf for books and magazines.

Right: Painted fabric panels can be pulled across when the table is used for entertaining. Below: A screen divides the two areas in this room.

Dining area furniture

Dining rooms in small houses need adaptable furniture – extendable tables, folding chairs, sideboards, and shelving for storage. And, as the dining area is so often part of the living room or kitchen, dining furniture needs to fit in with other furniture. Remember that mealtimes should be enjoyable and relaxing – so make sure the chairs are comfortable.

Left: Slipcovers will update favorite chairs that have seen better days. Right: Family treasures or thrift-store finds will look good in the corner of a country kitchen.

Choose a table to suit the space available. A round table will seat more people in comfort and takes up the same floor area as a square one. A gateleg table is useful when space is in short supply – it folds down to a slim size and will sit against a wall when not in use.

An extendable table makes sense if you like to entertain but have limited space. Loose leaves mean that the extra leaf has to be kept somewhere when not in use. Integral leaves make a table heavy, but you do save the extra storage space which may be put to better use. See how the table extends and note the position of the legs in relation to where everyone sits. A central pedestal won't be in anyone's way.

Whatever you decide, the most important thing is to choose a table to suit your needs. For example, a large table in the kitchen may take up space, but gives you an extra work surface.

Garden furniture can also double as dining furniture and is a reasonably inexpensive way of furnishing a dining room. Garden chairs are useful for extra seating

In a small house, furniture needs to be adaptable, and storage is all-important. This attractive painted settle doubles as a neat and roomy storage box for a set of folding chairs.

and slip covers will make them appear more substantial.

Comfortable chairs are vital, or no one will want to linger at the dinner table: seats should be deep and not cut into the backs of legs at the front edge; chair backs should give support without being too rigid. Upholstered seats and backs are the most comfortable and are best suited for a shared living room. Wipe-clean chairs are advisable in a kitchen/dining room, but add washable seat cushions for extra comfort.

Slipcovers or tie-on seat cushions will bring new life to old chairs. They also provide an opportunity to make a color link with other decoration in the room.

Whatever chairs you choose, sit on them before you buy. And make sure they fit neatly under your table or they will waste a lot of valuable floor space.

Dining area lighting

Lighting is very important in a dining area. Too much light and you feel as if you are under a spotlight – too little and you can't see what's on the table. The balance needs to be just right to set a relaxing mood.

It is difficult to light two areas in the same room for different purposes, but it can be done.

A rise-and-fall pendant will give a pool of light which can be focused onto the table, while candles combined with background lighting such as wall lights, table lamps and uplighters will create a more intimate mood.

If your dining area is part of the kitchen the lighting may be too bright, because you need more light to prepare food than you do to eat it. One solution is to have kitchen and dining lights on separate switches, preferably dimmers, so that the kitchen lights can be turned off – or at least dimmed – when you eat. Or switch off just the main kitchen lights and leave on the under-cupboard lights.

The focal point of any dining area is the table, so intimate lighting is needed here. A rise-and-fall pendant will cast an intimate pool of light on the surface and can be pushed up when the table is not in use. To prevent dazzling your guests, bulbs should not be visible from seating positions. If they are, use crown silvered bulbs.

Candles are a must for that intimate feel, but they can be a bit dim just on their own. Use candles on the table, but keep them below eye-level or you and your guests will be continually peering around them to keep conversation going.

Keep light fittings over the table low, so guests will not feel they are in the spotlight.

Dining area flooring

Dining-room floors should be practical and hardwearing, yet comfortable underfoot. Always go for something that is easy to keep clean, but don't forget the look. A dining-room floor can be somewhere to experiment, so why not try out your painting and stenciling skills?

If your dining area is part of the kitchen, then you will have the same flooring throughout. If you still have the original floorboards, you can paint them and then seal them with varnish and they will be easy to keep clean. Or treat them as a canvas, and stencil around the dining table and chairs to distinguish the dining area from the kitchen area. Laminated wood and wood-effect vinyl are also simple to clean.

Linoleum is perfect for kitchen-diners as it can be cut to almost any design. To distinguish the dining area, simply take a pattern – maybe from curtains or wallpaper – and transfer it to the floor.

Quarry and terracotta tiles are fine for a country-style kitchen, but they can be expensive and need a certain amount of upkeep; ceramic tiles will do the same job and are much cheaper. Whatever tiles you choose, you need to ensure that they are laid on a solid, level base. The drawbacks with these types of hard floor are that they are cold underfoot and anything dropped on them will usually break. A heavy object might also break the tiles.

When the living and dining areas are shared, go for something comfortable and stylish that will not show the dirt too much. Again, a wooden floor is attractive and practical, and a couple of large rugs will help to define each area and make the room look more homey. Wall-to-wall carpet is also popular, and if it is your choice, pick one with an inbuilt stain protector to extend its life. You can also have an existing carpet cleaned and then protected. Seagrass is an alternative to carpet. Woven from natural grass fibers, it can be made into rugs or fully fitted. It creates a good transition from living to dining areas, but be careful what you spill on it, as the weave can be difficult to clean.

China

It is convenient to store china, glass, and flatware close to the dining table. If the space is available, a sideboard with shelves and drawers is a good idea. This will also provide a surface from which to serve food and drinks. A Swedish-style plate rack (see page 126) keeps plates at hand and is a good way of showing them off if you have a particularly decorative collection.

Open shelves are versatile and can store and display dishes successfully. Organize china and glass neatly – an arrangement of plates or bowls can be as pleasing to the eye as a favorite painting.

Basic white dinner plates will take you through any social occasion. Buy bone china, which will last a lifetime and longer, while earthenware will chip and wear relatively quickly. White china can be mixed easily with other colors and patterns. Try to keep to a color theme – blue and white works well, and there is a lot of this color combination around.
Yard sales and thrift stores are good sources of cheap and unusual china and glass.

If you have old pieces that you want to match, contact the manufacturer as the design may still be in production. Or try one of the china-match services which you will find in the classified-ad

Choose a color theme when starting a china collection. Blue and white are eternal and mix well with other colors.

Tableware

The right china and flatware should take you through any occasion. Choose a dinner service that you can add to. Basic white china, or a design from one of the well-known companies, can be supplemented with bright earthenware to give it a new look. The same goes for glassware and flatware – choose readily available designs and build your collection at your own pace. If you choose plain, classic tableware, it is much easier to change the look with colored tablecloths, napkins, and candles.

sections in the back of home interest magazines. They may specialize in just one or two manufacturers, but it is worth a try if you have fallen in love with a particular design.

Caring for china

To avoid scratching plates when they are stacked, lift them from the top; don't pull them out from the bottom. Most new china is dishwasher-proof, but if you are buying old piece,s wash them by hand. Hard-water deposits can be removed with diluted vinegar.

Glasses

Wine glasses should be large enough for you to swirl the wine around the bowl to release the smell and flavor, without it ending up in your lap! Tulip-shaped glasses are the best for wine, but they should be easy to drink from full or nearly empty.

On the table, have a glass for red, a glass for white, and a glass for water. Serve cocktails and liqueurs in small glasses – you can always use the same one as long as it is washed in between.

Store glasses in a cupboard, on their stem – they will pick up any smell in the cupboard if they are stored upside down. If the glasses have not been used for a while, wash them before they are used.

Flatware

When buying flatware, hold the pieces in your hand and feel how comfortable they are. Does the handle sit well in the palm of the hand? Does the weight and size feel right? Are there any sharp bits that will irritate under constant use?

Choose a design that has a full selection of pieces. Start with basic knives, forks, soup spoons, and teaspoons, and add to them as you can afford to. Alternatively, mix different designs together as long as the pieces are roughly the same size and weight.

Stainless steel is the most hardwearing material for flatware. Look for the figures 18/10 or 18/8. These refer to the percentage of chromium and nickel (which increase resistance to stains and corrosion) added to the base metal.

Silver-plated flatware has a thin layer of silver over a base metal and is more expensive than stainless steel. Most of it comes in traditional designs that are still around today, so if you inherit solid-silver or silver-plated flatware, the chances are that you will still be able to find pieces to match.

Acrylic-handled flatware comes in many pretty colors and can add sparkle to a table setting, but it is usually only available in the four basic pieces – knife, fork, tablespoon, and teaspoon.

Left: Unusual flatware adds the final touch to a table setting and will pull a theme together.
Right: Beautifully presented china can be as pleasing to the eye as a favorite picture.

Project 16

Night lights from tin cans

Candles at the table always create an intimate atmosphere and make an unusual centerpiece. These night lights are based on Shaker-style punched-tin lanterns.

1 Take the top off the can using a traditional can opener with a butterfly side handle that leaves the rim intact.

2 Cut the tracing paper to match the depth and circumference of the can. Work out the pattern on the tracing paper – keep to simple shapes that are easily identifiable, such as stars, hearts, or fish.

You will need
● Plain tin cans of varying sizes, used for fruit or vegetables (not soft drinks)
● Tracing paper
● Masking tape
● Drill with a metal bit
● Candles

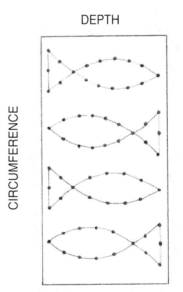

DEPTH

CIRCUMFERENCE

4 Using a metal bit on your drill, drill holes where you have marked the dots. Be careful not to let the can or drill slip. The can may buckle under the pressure, but it is easily straightened.

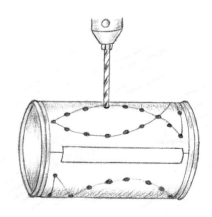

3 Mark dots at intervals along the outline of the shapes – not too close together – and tape the tracing-paper image around the outside of the can.

Project 17

Painted glasses

Paint glasses to match your china or decorate them for a special occasion such as a birthday or wedding. Glass paint is reasonably permanent, so wash glasses by hand using a soft cloth or sponge and do not rub the design.

You will need
- Glasses
- Pearlescent glass paint
- Paintbrushes

1 Wash the glasses in hot soapy water and dry with a glass cloth. Remove any glue from price labels with denatured alcohol.

2 Use one color at a time or the paints will run into each other. To make the spots, dot blobs of paint and leave to dry.

3 Outline the spots in a different color and leave to dry. Continue building up the layers of paint until you get the intensity of color that you want. I gave these glasses four coats of paint.

Variation:
Cut shapes from self-adhesive plastic to stick on the glass. Trace numbers from a book to encourage children to count, or cut thin strips of different colors and stick them on in a continuous spiral.

Project 18
Pleated tablecloth for a round table

Tablecloths never seem to fit round tables properly. This pleated cloth fits perfectly and uses about two yards of fabric, depending on the size of the table. Be sure to choose contrasting complementary fabrics for the cloth and internal pleats.

You will need
- 2 yards fabric
- 20 inches contrasting fabric
- Matching thread
- Sewing machine

1 Measure the dimensions of the table top – the one I used had a 41-inch diameter and 10½-foot circumference. The drop of the tablecloth is to be 8 inches.

2 Cut a circular piece of fabric for the table top, adding a ¾- inch hem allowance. Cut four rectangles of the same fabric, 32¾ inches x 8¾ inches for the drop.

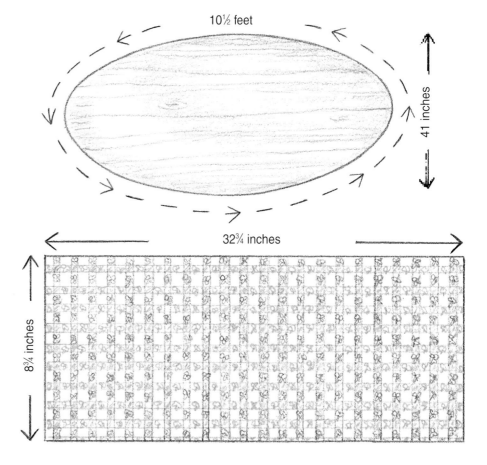

10½ feet

41 inches

32¾ inches

8¾ inches

Also cut four 8¾-inch squares of fabric from a contrasting fabric for the inverted pleats.

3 Join all eight pieces together alternately, giving each seam a ½ inch allowance.

4 With right sides facing, place a pin vertically in the center of the contrasting fabric pleat and fold the border fabric in toward the pin and then back on itself. Pin the fabric in place and repeat on the other side. Pin the other three pleats this way.

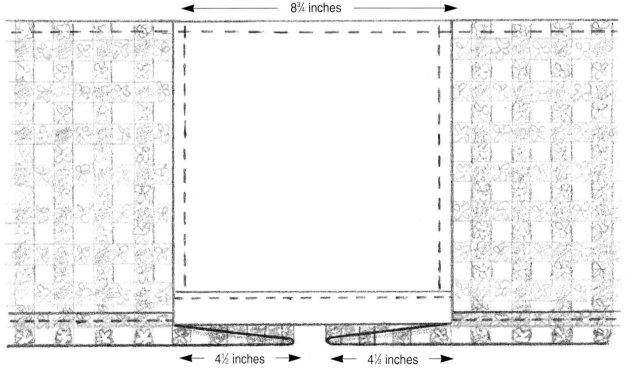

5 Pin and baste the border onto the circular top and sew in place.

6 Turn up a ½-inch hem and press. The cloth should fit the table exactly.

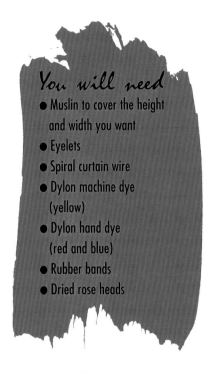

You will need

- Muslin to cover the height and width you want
- Eyelets
- Spiral curtain wire
- Dylon machine dye (yellow)
- Dylon hand dye (red and blue)
- Rubber bands
- Dried rose heads

Project 19

Gauze curtains with eyelet heading and dried rose heads

If your dining area is part of another room, a gauze curtain can isolate it and create an intimate feel. With this wire-and-eyelet heading, it can stretch from wall to wall where there is no other means of support.

1 Measure the drop and width of the curtains. Most gauze comes in 36-inch widths, so you will need to sew several widths together.

2 Following the manufacturer's instructions, dye all the gauze yellow with a machine dye in the washing machine. Leave it to dry.

3 Cut the gauze to the required drop, and place the cut lengths on top of each other. They must be dyed together to get the same line when they are sewn together.

4 Mix the red hand dye in a bucket, following the manufacturer's instructions. Dip the bottom third of all the fabric pieces into the red dye and leave for the required length of time (put the top half of the fabric in a plastic bag to prevent splashing). Hang up to dry.

5 Mix a small amount of blue hand dye. Gather a handful of fabric about 12 inches from the bottom of each piece of gauze, where it has been dyed red, and tie a rubber band around each piece. This will give you a tie-dye effect.

6 Dip the gauze in the blue dye and leave it for the required amount of time. Drip dry and then take the rubber bands out.

7 Sew together two lengths of gauze to make one curtain. Turn over a 1¼-inch hem at the top and a ½-inch hem at the bottom of the curtain.

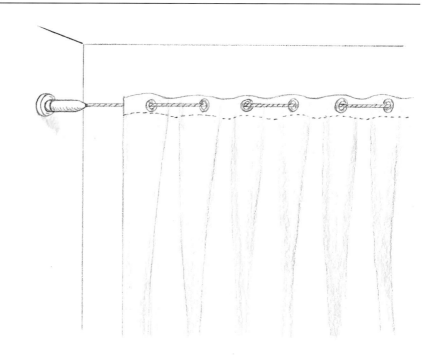

8 Figure out the position of the eyelets, about every 6 inches. Position the two sides of the eyelet on each side of the gauze. Hit the top piece with a hammer so that it cuts through the fabric and snaps together with the bottom piece. Place the eyelets on a stable surface when you hit them. It is best to have a practice run first.

9 Repeat the eyelet heading on the other curtain.

10 Fit the curtain wire to one wall. Thread the curtains onto the wire and anchor the wire track on the opposite wall, then pull tight.

11 Sew or pin the dried rose heads onto the yellow part of the curtains.

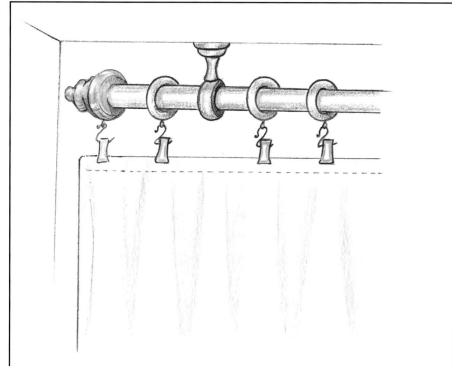

Variation

This idea will work just as well with a curtain pole attached to the ceiling. Make sure you find the joists to screw into. You could leave the finials off the curtain pole so that the curtain hangs as close to the wall as possible. Leave the eyelet heading off and use curtain clips instead to hook onto the curtain rings.

Project 20
Swedish-style plate rack

It is a pity to keep pretty plates unseen in a cabinet. This Swedish-style plate rack keeps them on show and at hand for when you need them.

You will need
- ¼-inch thick plywood
- 1 x 4-inch softwood
- 1 x 2-inch softwood
- ¾-inch dowel
- Craft glue
- Wood screws
- Brads
- Carpenter's level
- Awl

1 Cut the plywood to the overall size of the plate rack, in this case 31½ x 55 inches. (Check the size of the plates you plan to put into the rack first.) Cut a length of 1 x 4-inch softwood to 55 inches and screw and glue to the front bottom edge of the plywood to make the bottom shelf.

2 Cut three 31½-inch lengths of 1 x 4 inch to make the uprights that hold the dowels. On one, mark the position of the dowels, about 1¼ inches in from the outside edge. Place all three pieces on top of each other and drill the two ¾-inch holes through all three, to make sure that all the holes are in the same place.

3 Pin the supports with brads and glue then onto the plywood back; then screw to the bottom shelf from underneath.

4 To make the ledges for the plates to sit on, cut six pieces of 1 x 2-inch softwood to fit between the vertical supports. Mark the lengths of the ledges by measuring them against the inside of the frame.

5 Leaving enough space to put small pitchers underneath, mark the position of the first and second ledges with a pencil. Measure up from the bottom shelf so that the shelf and ledges are parallel.

6 Drill through the plywood, between the two horizontal lines marking the place of the ledges. Put the ledges in position

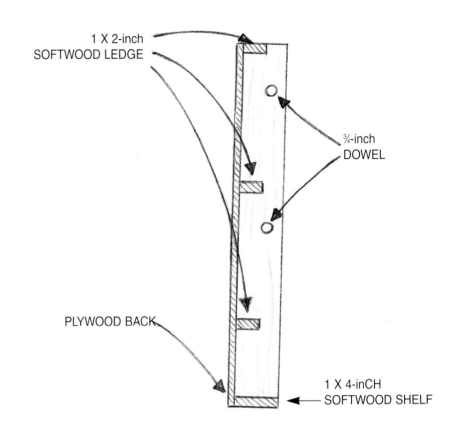

Plate rack cross section

1 X 2-inch
SOFTWOOD LEDGE

¾-inch
DOWEL

PLYWOOD BACK

1 X 4-inCH
SOFTWOOD SHELF

and puncture them with an awl, through the holes you have just drilled, from the reverse side of the plywood back. Screw into position.

7 Mark the two lengths of the dowel against the frame.

8 Push the dowels through the holes and glue before positioning. Tap through with a hammer against a small block of wood.

9 Fill all the holes with wood putty. Paint and varnish.

10 To mount it on the wall, drill through the plywood to the wall with screws close to the four corners and on each side of the center vertical, top and bottom.

Plate rack dimensions

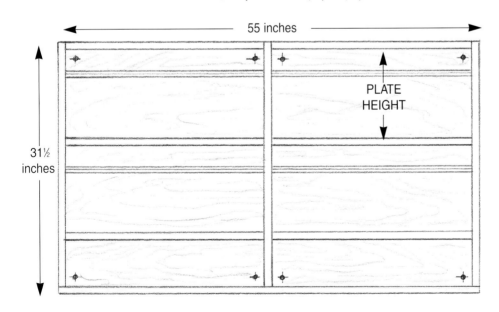

55 inches

31½ inches

PLATE HEIGHT

Likes/dislikes

When you walk into your living room, which things immediately strike you as good or bad features? Make a note of these now – even if you are not sure yet how you would set about improving them. It will help if you can remember what you loved or hated about the room on the day you moved in. First impressions count, but as time passes, you can get used to the most frightful things, and the true horror can fade in front of your eyes.

A good design is one that is well balanced – in other words, no one thing in a room should strike you the moment you walk through the door. Each element of the room should complement the other elements. Visitors should walk into your room and comment on how attractive the whole room is, not just the wallpaper or carpet.

Do not despair if your list of "hates" is twice the length of your list of "likes". Later you will see how plenty of problems need not be problems at all – or can be disguised at least. Sometimes even the most unfortunate of features can be transformed into something full of character, if not beautiful.

Is the room light or dark?

If your living room doesn't get much natural light, you will need to bear that in mind when it comes to choosing your color scheme. It is usual to want to create as much impression of light in a room as possible, although if you feel you

Chapter five

Your living room

If you are serious about creating a wonderful living room, you need to go about it in a serious manner. That is not to say the project won't be fun – it will be – but you will also save time and money if you approach the redesign of your front room as a professional would.

An interior designer would start by discussing your living room and how it is used before looking at a color card. Of course you want the room to look great – but you need it to be practical, too. Professional designers refer to this first crucial stage as "taking the brief" – when they take detailed notes about the room, what it is used for, and what you hope to get out of it.

Why not sit down, take a long look at your room and take your own brief? You can ask other members of the family for their input at this stage, too – that way you can be sure that everyone's expectations are considered.

This approach may seem excessive if you were just planning to slap on some fresh paint, but it will really help you to get the best out of your room.

are fighting a losing battle, you may consider emphasizing a room's darker, more dramatic nature. Perhaps you work long hours and only use your living room when it is dark anyway, in which case a shortage of natural light is not a problem.

Think about how you might improve upon the light in the room. If your budget will extend to it, you may want to consider adding another window – or perhaps you could replace a solid door with a glazed one. These are decisions that should be made at the planning stage – not once the wallpaper is up on the walls.

If the room is naturally light, you will have more of a free hand when it comes to decorating. However, it may be that you have large windows that dominate the room and you need to direct the focus of the room elsewhere.

Which way does the room face?

This will affect the light that a room receives. A room that faces north, east, or northeast will usually receive a colder light than one that faces south, west, or southwest, so it will need a warmer color scheme to make it feel more comfortable (see page 135).

How do you use your living room?

Consider what you do in your living room and what should be incorporated into your new-look room to make it practical and comfortable as well as stylish.

The following questions may point you in the right direction:

Who will be using the living room? Is it a place where people read or do particular hobbies, and will they need special seating, tables, or lighting?

Do you watch television here? The set will need to be positioned appropriately, bearing in mind how light reflects off the screen and where the chairs are.

Will your hi-fi be in this room? You may want to consider a storage unit for the hi-fi. If so, you should check that there are enough sockets for both this and the TV.

Do you need somewhere for drinks?

Is there adequate heating? Will you want to install a fire or radiators? You may want to consider installing a dummy fireplace simply to provide an attractive focus to the living room.

Is the lighting adequate? Does one person like to read while another watches TV, works, or dozes? You may need different types of lighting around the room and plenty of sockets (see Living room lighting, page 143).

Do you need more storage for books? Consider where you could put this and if you want your books on view or hidden away.

Do you have personal collections you would like to display? If you collect plates or

If you have a collection to display, you need to consider the best way of doing it, even if that simply means arranging pictures on the floor.

ornaments, you will need shelf space and maybe appropriate lighting to show them off.

Does the living room also serve as a dining room? Think about creating a special dining area. Perhaps it could have a different type of floor covering, be cut off by a screen, and given subdued lighting.

What is your budget? One of the most crucial parts of the brief. Before you head for the hardware store, it is important that you set a top figure, allowing about ten percent for any unforeseen expenditures – there are sure to be some once work begins.

Then it is up to you to juggle the budget according to your own priorities. If you simply must have a luxurious wool carpet, that's fine, but it may mean you have to opt for cheaper wallpaper and lighting. Take another look at your personal brief and decide which of your planned changes are the most important to you.

Once you start your research into furniture and furnishings, keep a note of the projected cost of each item, then add it all up before you buy. That way, you can be sure that you keep within your means.

Making the most of what you've got

Few people are lucky enough to be able to start from scratch each time they decorate. The majority have to make the most of existing carpets, worn curtains, and sofas which have seen better days. We also have to live with the existing shape and structure of the house – whether we like it or not. There is only so much knocking down of walls, lowering of ceilings, and extending it out that one house can take – and when you are working to a tight budget, drastic changes such as these are likely to be completely out of the question.

Do not despair. Your living room can be transformed with just a few clever decorating tricks – and none of them costs a fortune or requires building work. In fact, many living rooms with "problem" features eventually become the most interesting and pleasing rooms of all.

Coping with existing furnishings

While taking your brief, you will have listed the things that bother you most about your living room as it stands. You will also have begun to work out your budget. Again, it is up to you to juggle your priorities. If opting for paint rather than wallpaper means you can afford to ditch the awful carpet, then go for it! Do a bit of research before you start and you may find that you can do some things for less money than you anticipated. You might find a carpet remnant that fits your living room perfectly (especially if it is a small room), or you may spot a special offer on the ideal wallpaper. You never know, miracles sometimes happen...

Inevitably, however, there will be several things that you cannot replace and will have to put up with for a few more years. Here's how to make the most of them:

The old sofa: Having an old sofa or armchair re-upholstered can sometimes cost as much as buying a new one, so unless the sofa is of a reasonable quality and you are happy with the shape and size of it, it is probably not worth considering. What might be worthwhile, however, is finding someone to make slipcovers. They are a cheaper option and can be taken off for washing and even changed to suit the seasons. Some companies offer washable elasticized covers which, with a bit of manipulating, can look as if they were made to fit your sofa. If you want to spend as little money as possible on revamping your couch, try covering it with plenty of large scatter cushions artfully placed to hide the worn patches. Or give it a completely new look by covering it with a throw. Plenty of stores now stock a good selection of afghans, but you can get something unique – and a better fit – if you make it yourself. Turn to page 147 for instructions on how to make a customized throw.

The dreadful carpet: Your living room is likely to be a high-traffic area – being used for entertaining and relaxing more than any other room in the house – so you need flooring that can take the strain.

Carpet remains one of the largest investments you will have to make, so it can be depressing to be faced with an existing carpet that is tacky or worn. Ripping it up is not your only option, however. If the problem is simply a few bare patches, you could arrange your furniture to cover the worst of them and invest in a rug or two. If the whole carpet is beyond hope, you could buy a cheap rug large enough to cover most of it and then artfully site your furniture over the surrounding area.

Check the state of the floor beneath your carpet. You may be lucky and discover some perfect floorboards or parquet just waiting to be renovated. Bare varnished boards can look really chic as well

You can give old furniture a new lease on life without spending a fortune.

as being hardwearing and cheap (see page 144).

An ugly fireplace: Old gas heaters can be particularly unattractive, so, unless yours is in constant use, consider ways of concealing it – perhaps with a folding screen or a light piece of furniture. If it is not often used, why not take it out completely? Original period fireplaces are often reasonably priced at architectural salvage yards and they can be installed very cheaply if you don't necessarily want to light a fire in them.

Shabby furniture: It is amazing how you can transform a plain, shabby piece of furniture with just a little time and attention. As long as the basic shape is appealing, it is easy to turn it into something special. Look at your old tables and chests of drawers. Could the handles or feet be changed? How would they look if the paint or varnish were stripped off and restored? It is well worth experimenting – after all, what have you got to lose?

Coping with structural problems

Even the most perfect houses have their shortcomings, although many of them are subject to individual taste: one person's "cramped" is another person's idea of "cozy", for instance.

You may not be able to change the structure of your living room, but you can alter the impression the room gives by emphasizing certain aspects and concealing others.

Here are some of the most common problems and how to rectify them:

Ceilings: People tend to lose interest when it comes to ceilings. They spend ages deliberating over walls, floors, and furniture – then simply slap white latex above it all. Using colour on the ceiling can help you create the look you are after. (Turn to page 135 for more tips on color.)

Making it lower: If the ceiling is too high, paint it a darker, warmer color than the walls or, if you are feeling bold, use a textured paper. Add a picture rail and extend the ceiling color down to the rail, and perhaps decorate the walls in horizontal stripes.

Making it higher: Modern houses with their lower ceilings usually have the opposite problem. In this instance, there is an argument for using white paint as it will make the ceilings recede from view. But why not be a bit more adventurous? You can achieve the same receding effect by painting the ceilings in a cool color, such as a pastel shade, lighter than the walls below. You can also use pattern to achieve the effect you want. Painted vertical stripes or a vertically striped wallpaper will accentuate the height of the walls and appear to lift the ceiling up.

Making the living room larger: Most people feel that they have not got enough space, but you can fool the eye into thinking that a room is larger than it is by playing with the scale of the

furniture in the room. If you are replacing furniture, opt for smaller and lower pieces, such as neat two-seat sofas, little wicker armchairs, and tiny coffee tables that do not overpower the room.

Emphasize the width of the room with shallow, wide pieces placed along the walls and choose wall-to-wall carpet, which naturally draws the eye to the corners. Pick light colors for your decoration and furnishings and avoid anything but the smallest of patterns.

Making the living room wider: If you have a double living room where two adjacent rooms have been converted into one, it can easily adopt the appearance of a tunnel – especially if there are only two windows, one at each end. You should aim to draw those two ends of the room inward and break up the floor between them.

Choose warm, bold colors for the ends of the room, especially for the curtains, which when drawn will bring the room "together" more. Most important, avoid placing all your furniture along the walls. Try to break up the room by placing two small sofas opposite each other, one in the middle of the room, or by using small tables to create islands of interest.

The color wheel

Interior designers often refer to a color wheel – a basic way of demonstrating how certain colors mix together to make other colors (red and blue produce purple, for example). The wheel can be divided into halves – one half containing the warm colors (red, red/orange, orange, yellow/orange, and yellow, and their various tints and shades) and the other the cool colors (green, blue/green, blue, and blue/violet, and their shades).

The warm colors are also known as "advancing" colors, as they tend to make walls look closer to you. Cool colors on the other hand, are referred to as "receding", as they have the effect of moving away from you.

Choosing a color

Using this basic theory, you can create a living room that looks either bigger or smaller than it really is, lighter or darker and either warmer or cool and airy.

Remember that the darker shades of any color, including green and blue, will make your living room look smaller than a pastel shade. Try not to let the size of your living room deter you from the warmer or darker shades completely, however. A small room that gets enough light can look stunning in a rich orange or deep green –

Be as bold as you dare. Once you have gained color confidence, stylish and stimulating schemes could transform your home.

Living room color

Ask people what confuses them most when it comes to designing their homes and the answer is likely to be color. Choosing which colors go with which and then putting together fabric and wallpaper samples usually has the effect of sending most people back to the can of white latex. In years gone by, this wasn't such a problem, but current trends are encouraging us to be bold and daring with the brightest shades. So how do you gain the confidence to put together the living room of your dreams?

The first step is to learn a little theory. It may sound boring and technical, but once you understand how colors "work", the decisions will be much easier. This approach may seem excessive if you were planning only to slap on some fresh paint and rearrange the furniture, but it will really help you to create a stunning room scheme.

especially if you tend to use the room more often in the evening, subtly lit by artificial light.

Think about the kind of effect you want to achieve. For traditional impact, go for a deep red or library green; for modern chic opt for mauves, lime greens, and even orange. Or perhaps you would prefer something more subtle, such as a pastel pink or mint.

Different colors have been proven to have certain psychological effects. If you see your living room as a retreat, somewhere to relax and be yourself, then go for blue, the color of harmony and peace. If you want a living room that livens you up each morning, try yellow – a joyful, sunny color associated with creative energy and power. If you fancy something more traditionally warm, you could go for red. But be warned, red is an appetite-inducing color!

Although some color schemes use just one color and then accessorize it with various shades of the same hue, most tend to pick out an accent color from the opposite side of the color wheel to add a dash of interest.

If you choose a mainly blue living room, add a few yellow pillows to your sofa and pick out some yellow or orange in the drapes or on a vase for extra sparkle. If you fancy dramatic red walls, try going for lampshades in an equally deep shade of green. A living room offers plenty of opportunity for adding flashes of contrasting color in pillows, rugs, and lampshades – as well as more obvious statements in the larger pieces, such as the sofa and carpet.

If the concept of decorating in red and green or bright blue and yellow is still rather hard for you to handle, turn to nature for inspiration and proof of success. Think of a bright-blue iris, its center shot with yellow, or a green holly bush laden with red berries. Nature never gets it wrong.

Using existing furnishings for inspiration

If you are still stuck for ideas or confused about where to start, existing furnishings that need to be incorporated into the scheme may help rather than hinder.

If your sofa has to stay put, decide whether you would like it to play a large or minor part in the color scheme. If you would rather play it down, take your main color from the opposite side of the color wheel and use the sofa merely as an accent. If you decide to use it as the major color in the room, then look for paint or wallpaper in a similar shade and select an accent color – or two – from the opposite side of the color wheel.

Using color for definition

A living room tends to be the focus of a variety of different activities, from studying to relaxing or dining. Indeed, as the pressure on housing space grows and more people live in studio-style apartments, the demands put on this one room are increasing.

Use color and pattern to emphasize the various functions of the room and give different areas an appropriate look.

In a living/diner, try decorating the dining area of the room in a different color – or in the same shade as the living areas, but using a different pattern. An alcove, with desk and bookshelves, can become a designated study area simply by giving it a different splash of color.

Natural living

If your furniture and accessories are largely wood or made from stripped, natural materials, you may choose a neutral scheme to complement them. The key here is to extend the range of colors in your furnishings to cream, ocher, coffee – and maybe shades of gray. Black is a neutral color, but it can look harsh and should be used very sparingly.

These neutral shades, especially white and black, can be used in most color schemes as an extra accent color. See how a black cast-iron fireplace sits well in any scheme, as does white woodwork.

Pattern and texture

A living room with a neutral color scheme relies on pattern and texture for extra interest. A natural room will never be boring if sisal flooring is combined with textured rugs, gauze at the window, silk pillows and a rough-hewn wooden coffee table. Use pattern and texture to enhance any color scheme, however bright and bold.

Planning on paper

To juggle furniture without breaking your back, do the initial planning on paper. You may have already drawn a floor plan when you took the measurements for carpet and so on. If not, do so now by transferring your measurements onto graph paper using a scale that allows you to fit your plan on an 8x10 sheet – 1:20 is normally adequate. Mark on it where your sockets are, where the radiator is, where the TV antenna is, the direction the doors open, and the position of the windows.

Now measure the pieces of furniture which are staying in the room. You do not need their heights, only the widths and depths (though you could keep a note of heights in case you need them later). Adapt these measurements to the same scale as the floor plan and cut them from squared paper. Write on each one what it is, so you don't get confused. Using your plan, you can play around with the positioning of the furniture until you reach the perfect compromise of style and practicality.

If you are planning to buy a new sofa or table and do not know how big it is going to be, leaf through a few catalogs. You'll soon get an idea of the average sizes of a two- or three-seater sofa and the sort of table you want, and you can use these sizes as rough guides.

Living room furniture

Living room furniture needs to be as comfortable as it is practical – and it has to look good, too. These are high demands, and it is worth taking time to plan and research thoroughly before buying.

Start by taking a good look at what you've already got and ascertain what else you need. Go back to your initial brief and look at how the room is used. This will dictate the type of furniture you buy and where it is positioned in the room. If the television can only go in one particular corner, then the sofa will need to be placed appropriately. Make sure you allow enough room for bookshelves, storage units, and pictures.

Selecting just the right armchair or sofa will make all the difference to your living room.

Once you are happy with the plan, or even just part of it, trace it complete with positioned furniture onto tracing paper and put it to one side. You may find you do several tracings, but then you can compare them to help you make your final decision.

Effective positioning

The way you place your furniture can alter the effect of the whole room, making it appear spacious or cluttered, traditional or quirky. While you move your furniture around your plan, think about how you can position it in a more interesting and imaginative way.

It is easy to slip into the habit of putting everything right up against the wall, with perhaps a coffee table as the only exception, but if your room has the space – and especially if it's a living/dining room – you can try to create little islands of interest to break it up. Sofas do not need to have their backs up against the wall: try bringing them into the middle of the room instead, positioning two either back to back or facing each other to make a more inviting and comfortable seating area.

Chairs do not need to face the center of the room either – group some around a small table to create an intimate area within the larger room. Use screens, chests, and tables to break up expanses of floor and experiment with the positioning of desks – could they face into the room instead of the wall? You may find that by breaking the rules you make more efficient use of your space.

Practical positioning

Practical comfort and safety should be remembered when you play with your plan – especially if you have children. You need a certain amount of space between each piece of furniture and between furniture and a wall in order to pass comfortably between them. Check that there is room to pull a chair back or to circle a table, that heads won't be banged on overhead shelves, and that there will be no trailing cords.

Choosing a sofa or armchair

Deciding on the fabric of your sofa or armchair is just part of the process of choosing the chair itself. The next decision concerns the style – although you may have considered what sort of look you want, think about the practicalities of the style as well.

Do you tend to relax on the sofa alone or with your partner and/or children? If the whole family tends to gather on a sofa, you'll need one large enough to cope – or would two small sofas be better than one large one? Do you tend to sit on it, or do you prefer to stretch out?

If one person likes to stretch out and another sit, you'll need one long sofa and one armchair. Does anyone in the family have a back problem, or are there any elderly members of the family? If so, they won't appreciate a design which is hard to raise themselves out of. Check the comfort of a chair by sitting on it in the store in the manner that you would at home.

An attractive screen effectively separates a practical working area from a comfortable living room. You could use such a screen to create a separate dining area, too.

There is no point in resting your seat on that seat for a few seconds, then jumping up and declaring it to be fine. Ignore curious onlookers and relax into the chair. The upholstery should support you without sagging or being too rigid. Are the small of your back and your neck comfortably supported, and are the arms of the chair at a good height?

If your house doesn't have a spare room, you may want to consider a sofabed, which is as comfortable as a normal sofa and makes a good occasional bed, too. The cheaper models provide just a mattress on the floor, but most open out onto legs with a mattress. The quality of the mattresses can vary considerably, along with the price, so consider carefully how often it will be used as a bed, compare the different types for comfort and then make your decision.

Finally, don't feel you have to buy a three-piece set – or indeed any matching upholstery. A living room looks more effective if the upholstery has been mixed and matched with different styles of chairs and sofa. Pick out one or two colors that complement your scheme and look out for patterns that incorporate them. Don't be nervous about combining checks and stripes. If the shades are right, it will work. All it takes is a little confidence in your color skills.

Covering your living room windows

The way you cover your windows will set the tone of your living room and indeed of the whole house – for curtains and blinds play a large part in how your home looks from the outside, too.

Living room window dressings are important for both style and practicality – probably more so than in any other room of the house. If you use the living room during the day, you need to make the most of available light. Additionally, if you spend most evenings in your living room, you will want a sense of warmth and privacy, too. The best window dressings will offer all this – and look good at the same time.

Points to consider

There is a wealth of different styles to choose from, which makes the decision process harder than ever – but by focusing on your particular needs, you can make it a little easier. Before you even begin to look at fabrics, consider the following points: your window type and what it overlooks, the style or theme of your living room, and the amount of light the room receives.

The size and design of your windows will rule out certain designs immediately. Swags and tails sit less comfortably against modern picture windows, for example, while Venetian blinds do little for tiny casements. Full-length drapes usually need taller windows in order to look balanced, and grand swags require an imposing frame.

If your windows are small, or the living room doesn't get much light,

full drapes and impressive valances may be unsuitable simply because they block out what light there is and make the room too dark. Go for simple designs without low valances and use tiebacks to open up the window area. Or you could extend your pole or track beyond the window frame so that the drapes do not obscure the glass at all.

Equally there could be a need to protect your room from strong daylight or unwelcome eyes – particularly if your furnishings might fade in the sun or you have valuables on display. In this case, you will need to consider a combination of dressings, such as a flat blind for daytime and curtains for extra warmth at night.

Choosing a style:

Curtains: When drawn at night, curtains make a living room look cozy – and they help to keep it

warm, too, especially if they are given a thermal lining. Curtains finish and soften a window frame and provide added privacy in the evenings. However, if you want them to look luxurious they need a lot of fabric, so they can add up to be a rather expensive option.

There is a vast selection of headings and styles available, from tab heads for a simple Shaker style, and the more conventional pencil pleats, right through to swags, tails, rosettes, and shaped valances for traditional living rooms. Choose the finish to suit your room, or if that is beyond your means, consider a budget option from the following selection.

Blinds and shades: A cheaper option than drapes, blinds will minimize drafts and provide privacy. They also offer you more control over the amount of light you let into your living room. Roman, roll-upr, paper, and cane shades roll or fold up to allow more light to enter when you need it, while slatted blinds can also be adjusted to allow more or less daylight to filter through the slats. All of these styles offer a simple minimalist effect, but they can be dressed up and made to look much more decorative with any of the finishes outlined below.

Festoon and balloon shades are more luxurious, with ruched fabric

Effective window coverings needn't be costly. Draping fabric from swag holders is an inexpensive yet stylish option.

and ruffled edges, but can be too fussy and "feminine" for many living rooms.

Lace panels: Available ready-made in a variety of lengths, these allow light to filter attractively through the windows while offering privacy during the day – ideal if your living room is overlooked. A pretty alternative to conventional glass curtains, they can be combined with drapes or shades.

Shaped valances: Enjoying a well-deserved revival, the wooden valance is now available in an exciting choice of designs which can be covered in fabric or painted to match your scheme. Combined with simple drapes, it can be used to stunning effect, but it also works well on a small window as a dressing in its own right. Take care over the size of your valance though, and make sure it suits the scale of your window.

Dress curtains: If you never need to close your curtains – if they are combined with a shade or frame a door to the backyard for example – you needn't waste money on surplus fabric. Simply buy one width of fabric or enough to frame the sides of your window adequately. If the drapes are light enough, you may be able to get away with using a touch-and-close tape: one length is sewn to your drape and the other is stuck to the window frame, so you can simply "stick" your drapes up.

Quick, cheap, and easy

You do not need to spend a fortune to dress your windows with style – some of the simplest ideas are often the best:

Curtain clips: Just like normal curtain rings, but with a little clip at the bottom, these can be run along your pole in the usual way, then used for holding up pieces of fabric, gauze or lace – instant curtains with no sewing required. Curtain clips are ideal for minimalist living rooms or as a temporary measure.

Swag holders: These allow you to produce your own simple swagged valances without the formality or the cost of the real thing. All you have to do is feed a length of fabric through two of these curled metal brackets, mounted on each side of the top of your frame. The holders make it easy to create rosettes or let the fabric fall naturally so you can be as formal or relaxed as you please. Use them alone, over a shade or with drapes in a contrasting fabric.

Shaped valances can be made from composite board and then painted or covered in fabric to complement your color scheme.

Planning your lighting

It is important that you plan your lighting before you start to think about decorating. You don't want to ruin your new wallpaper just a week after it goes up.

Go back to your initial brief once more and think about what you and your family do in the living room. Do you use one end of the room as a formal dining area from time to time? It will need subtle lighting to create the perfect mood. Do you have paintings or prints that you would like to illuminate?

After you have planned the position of your furniture on your scaled paper plan, consider whether you have enough sockets for additional lamps in the appropriate places. If the armchair you like to read in is going in one corner, check that there is space and a socket to plug in a reading light next to it. You will need to have a lamp or light near or next to every seat in the room.

If you do use part of your living room as a dining area, treat that area separately and consider installing another pendant light (perhaps with a dimmer switch) above the table. Or you could restrict your permanent fixtures to the sides of the room, perhaps in the form of wall lights or table lamps, and light the table itself with candles.

Types of lighting

Ceiling lights: The most common light fixtures of all, these are

Living room lighting

It is surprising how much difference lighting can make to a room. The right lighting will transform a flat, uninteresting room in which people strain their eyes into an instantly more welcoming place with areas for reading, sleeping, studying, or watching television. Look at specialist lighting stores and at furnishing catalogs to get an idea of the sort of thing you would like and what would suit your room. You will need to decide whether to have modern or traditional-style lamps and where to put them.

usually in the center of the room and in the form of a pendant and shade, although there are plenty of other types of ceiling light to choose from. Think of the ceiling light as your starting point, then add extra lighting around the room. A pendant and shade will direct the light mostly downward and outward, according to the angle of the shade; spotlights allow you to direct light wherever it is needed; recessed downlighters shine a beam of light directly downward; while domed ceiling fixtures provide a diffused light.

Wall lights: These are a more subtle source of light than central ceiling fixtures. Traditional bracket lamps with small shades are perfect for Victorian-style living rooms. Modern wall lights are often uplighters, useful for adding attractive pools of light, but not ideal for reading. Picture lights also come into this category.

Table lamps: These can light the whole room or just add warm light to small areas of it without the overhead glare of a central ceiling light. They also allow you to control which areas are lit.

A table lamp casts a soft glow over attractive gold painted lettering in this room.

Floor lights: These are easy to move around the room, and are useful for both general and specific lighting. For positioning behind an armchair, look for a standard shade; for general lighting, go for an uplighter, and for directed pools of light, choose spotlights.

Candlelight: Don't keep candles purely for emergencies. They are a romantic and flexible light source, whether freestanding on a mantelpiece, on a wall sconce, or hung on a chandelier or in a lantern. They create an atmosphere electric light will never match.

Living room flooring

Choose the flooring for your living room to suit not only the room but also your lifestyle – and your budget. If the room is used regularly by a number of people and you have children or pets (or tend to be clumsy yourself), you will need a floor covering that can cope with the strain. If, however, you live alone and use the living room only to watch television or to entertain friends in the evenings, you may be able to get away with something more luxurious.

Hard or soft flooring

First you must decide whether you prefer hard flooring or carpet. A floor made of tiles, parquet, or wood strip will certainly be hardwearing as well as attractive. Wooden flooring is ideal for a traditional-looking living room, ranging from country or Shaker styles through to a simple Victorian look. Tiles are a more unusual (and costly) option for a living room, but can look cool and elegant or simple and rustic, depending on your choice of finish.

All hard flooring will take spills and act as a usefully neutral background to your furniture and furnishings – and it will last for years, however many times you want to change your color scheme. Hard floors are especially useful in living rooms that lead directly outside or onto the street. You will probably feel the need for a rug or two to soften the look and for extra warmth underfoot, and that – combined with the cost of wood or tiled flooring (plus underlay to stop rugs from slipping) – can be expensive.

Carpeting needs more maintenance – but it offers softness and warmth underfoot and a sense of wall-to-wall comfort. Its insulating qualities prevent footsteps from echoing around the house and, as there is such a wide range of materials and designs to choose from, there is sure to be one that will suit your color scheme and bank balance.

Choosing a carpet

Don't forget to budget for padding – a good pad increases the life of a carpet, makes it softer to walk on, and improves its insulating qualities. Foam-backed carpets are available as a cheaper alternative, but they are usually of inferior quality and their life span is accordingly much shorter.
If you are particularly worried about spills and damage, you could always try carpet tiles. They are made of heavy-duty materials and are easy to install and replace whenever necessary. The downside is that they come in limited colors.

When choosing your carpet, remember your color theory in order to achieve the effect you are aiming for. Reds, oranges, and yellows will have a warming effect, while blues and greens will cool the room down. Plain light-colored carpet laid wall-to-wall will make a room appear larger, whereas a heavily patterned carpet in darker colors will have the opposite effect – though to a lesser extent. Plain carpet shows every stain and piece of fluff, whereas patterns allow you to get away with more. Take some samples home to get an impression of how they will look in your room.

There is a third flooring option which falls somewhere between soft and hard. Natural matting made from vegetable fibers such as sisal, coir, jute, and seagrass is tough and hardwearing while offering some of the qualities of carpet – especially those varieties which combine natural fibers with the softness of wool and are laid over underlay. Natural flooring is generally available in neutral shades which complement any color scheme (although colored and patterned varieties are also on the market), and it suits traditional, rustic, and more contemporary living rooms.

Before you decide one way or the other, lift the existing carpet and check what is underneath. You may be lucky enough to discover some forgotten parquet or decent floorboards lurking below.

Before you rush off to rent a sander, however, do take up the carpet and check the whole floor – you may find that a small area is beyond repair.

Accessories

A living room without photographs, souvenirs, or memorabilia of any kind is little more than a shell, however beautifully decorated it may be. Accessories form the heart and soul of a room, introducing personality, humor, and interest.

There is an art to displaying your personal treasures – and choosing new ones to suit your redesigned living room – that ensures they earn the term "accessory" and do not become simply clutter.

Recognize a theme

If you have chosen a certain theme or style for your living room, it will be easy to complement it with accessories in a similar vein. You could decorate the walls of a Victorian living room with traditional prints, photographs, or paintings linked by a fabric bow. Finish a Shaker room with a peg rail hung with functional artifacts and some simple candle sconces. Enhance an ethnic setting with attractive rugs hung from wrought-iron curtain poles on the wall and perhaps a gilt-framed mirror. By turning to historical and geographical textbooks, you will find a wealth of inspirational ideas.

It is not necessary to stick rigidly to a theme or style, though. Your room will look even more interesting if you mix and match from across the years and oceans. Half the skill in decorating a home is in recognizing what will work together and what won't. Who cares if you put a Bakelite telephone in a Shaker-style room or a modern vase in a colonial farmhouse? If you like it, do it – it's your home, after all.

Above, and top: Displaying your collections, whether they are books, plates, or hats, gives a living room a personal feel and creates a lived-in, welcoming look.

Out with the old?

Buying new accessories is all well and good, but what about your existing pieces? The strong-hearted may quote William Morris ("Have nothing in your houses that you do not know to be useful or believe to be beautiful") and refer half their ornaments to the trash can. Indeed, unless you are an avid collector, you may wonder if your treasures really are worth displaying. Think again. After all, you have spent some time amassing them.

Accessories do not have to be large, valuable, or impressive to look the part, and even the simplest things gain credence and style once you have managed to arrange them successfully and to make an attractive display.

Think about what you would like to have around you when you go into the room, not just what visitors would like to see. Sort through your family photographs – perhaps there are a few special ones that you could group together in one area of the room. If you find any old sepia prints of your ancestors, these will look particularly special.

If you take a fresh look at your existing bits and pieces, you may begin to notice a common thread. Maybe you have several pots of the same house plant, or perhaps you have several different plants, all potted in the same style of earthenware. Perhaps you pick up a picture postcard every time you visit a museum and they are now

dotted around the house, or you can't resist buying candles and candlesticks whenever one catches your eye. You could mount the postcards on a colored background and put them together in one large frame. It need not be an expensive one – simple clip frames look very effective in the right setting. And what better place for a collection of candles and candlesticks than on the mantelpiece? Your collection will look even more effective in front of a mantel mirror. When the candles are lit, their reflections will sparkle, adding a touch of magic to the room.

By placing or hanging such things together, they become a collection immediately and worth a second glance. It may be that the only link is color, but that's fine. Position them together on a shelf or table, pin them on a peg board, or group them on the wall. Next time you buy anything new, you will have a clearer idea of what will work.

Create a welcome

The most welcoming living rooms appeal to all the senses. Think about what you see, hear, smell, and touch when you go into the room, and choose accessories accordingly to create the perfect atmosphere. These little things have as much impact as the carpet or drapes.

Fresh flowers are a must for both visual appeal and scent. Don't worry if you can't arrange them – casual displays in the simplest vessel will still look and smell the part and make a big difference.

Candles are also essential – especially if you do not have the luxury of a real open fire. Positioned around the room to create soft pools of romantic light, candles are a quick and easy way of creating a welcome after dark. Make them work doubly hard for you, and go for scented varieties – there is a wide range to choose from. Or put little night lights in an oil burner and heat fragranced essential oils. You don't even need a candlestick – a quick search around the house for alternatives such as terracotta pots, shallow dishes, or baskets packed with moss will only increase the imaginative impact of your lighting.

Stimulate the sense of touch with a pile of soft pillows, a chenille throw, a thick carpet to sink your toes into – and a warm radiator or a blazing fire.

You could even change your accessories to suit the seasons. Soft velvet cushions in jewel colors are perfect for brightening winter days. Swap them for cool, leafy green cottons and silks in pastel ice-cream colors for spring and summer.

And don't forget the sense of hearing. If you cannot guarantee pleasant birdsong just outside your window, use music to reflect or lift the mood.

Project 21

Sofa slipcover

By making your own slipcover, you not only guarantee that it will fit your sofa properly, but you also have more choice when it comes to fabrics – you could even make up some extra throw pillows from the same material to unite the color scheme around the room. A successful slipcover is cut generously so that it does not slip off whenever anyone sits on the sofa. It will drive you nuts if you are forever adjusting it. Press the slipcover after you've finished sewing and then experiment with it on the sofa to achieve the best look.

You will need:
- A measuring tape
- Enough material to cover your sofa generously (see Step 1)
- Bias binding in a contrasting color
- Matching thread and thread for basting
- Needles and pins

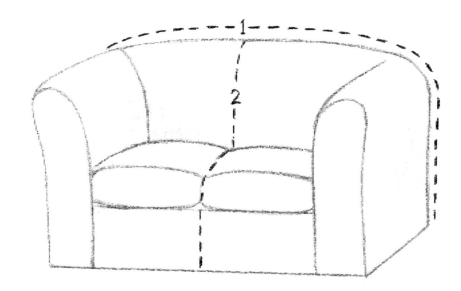

1 To estimate the amount of fabric you need, measure your sofa from floor to arm up the back, along the back and down over the arm to the floor again. Add on your pattern repeat plus 6 inches for working (measurement 1, the width you need). Then measure from the floor at the back, up the back and over the top, back down across the seat, and down to the floor. Add on your pattern repeat plus 6 inches for working (measurement 2, the length you need). As fabric comes in fairly narrow widths, you will find you need to work with at least two widths of your fabric.

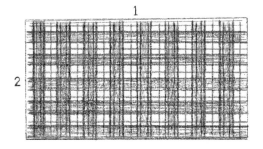

2 French seam your widths of fabric together to create a hardwearing join. This is done by placing the fabric wrong sides together and, with the pattern matching, pinning along the final join line. Tack along 12 mm (½ in) from the pin line with your raw edges level, then machine stitch along the tacking.

3 Trim the seam to 3 mm (⅛ in). Remove the pins, and press the seams open. Tack 6 mm (¼ in) from the first seam with your fabric folded right sides together, check the pattern match, and stitch along the tacking. Press the seam with the allowance to one side.

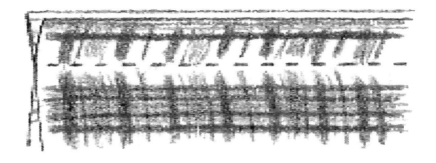

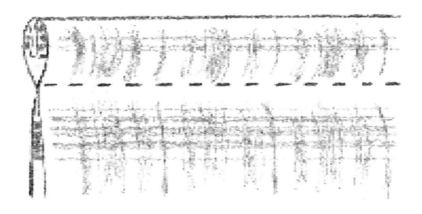

4 Estimate the amount of binding needed by measuring round all the edges of the throwover, plus 15 cm (6 in) for working. Press the binding off center then place it with the larger overlap on the wrong side of the fabric, and tack into place. When placing the binding to the corners, mitre the corners for a neat finish by folding the corners diagonally, trimming them off, then folding both edges in place before slip stitching the diagonal seam. Machine stitch along the tacking.

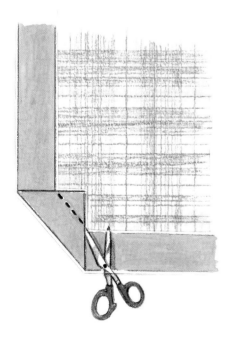

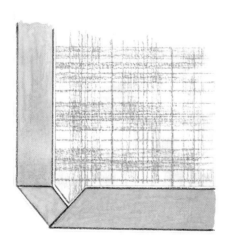

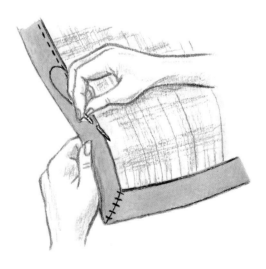

Project 22
Painted panels

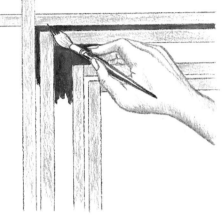

Y ou can add interest to a large expanse of wall by creating fake "panels" simply with paint. Use painted panels to make a feature of a picture or collection, to give added depth to a small window frame, or even to decorate a flat plain door. Once you get hooked on the idea, you may want to experiment with panels made from wallpaper borders to achieve an even more decorative look.

You will need:
- Plenty of masking tape
- Carpenter's level or plumb-line
- A pencil and yardstick
- Paint in a contrasting color to your main wall
- A small paint brush for touching up
- Paint in your main wall color, in case touching up is needed

1 Decide where you would like the panels to be and mark them carefully using a pencil, a yardstick as a guide and a carpenter's level and/or plumb-line. You will need to draw two

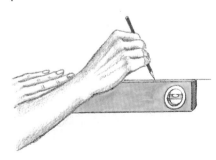

lines for each panel line to indicate the width of the finished painted line.

2 Stick masking tape down the outside of each drawn line to protect the surrounding wall. Take care to form sharp corners. Here both thick and thin lines have been used, so you will have some strips of masking tape close together and others wider apart.

3 Paint between the lines formed by the masking tape in a contrasting color to the main walls. Wait for the paint to dry, although not completely. Ideally, the wall should be dry enough to remove the masking tape without smudging the paint,

but not so dry that the paint dries and cracks over the adjoining ends.

4 Remove the masking tape carefully to reveal the painted panels. Be prepared for the masking tape to remove some of the old paintwork and have some of that paint and a fine brush on hand for touching up once the paint has dried completely.

Variation
The same technique can be used for creating a fake dado — it's cheaper and more interesting than the real thing.
- Draw a straight line running parallel to the floor at about the height of a chair back.
- Create a dado with masking tape and then paint between the guidelines.
- For best effect, use three paint colors — one for the dado itself and two different ones for above and below it.

Project 23

Decorating lampshades

Bring drab lampshades to life with your own unique design. Why settle for lampshades that will merely "do," when, with a little imagination, you can create shades that will complement and enhance your living-room scheme? Here I have used a simple stencil and a stamp to create two quite different looks.

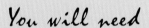

You will need

- A lampshade
  made of stiff fabric that
  will take paint, and is not
  too curved
- A stamp
- A small roller or sponge
- A tray or dish for paint

1 When you buy a stamp for this project, make sure that you choose one with a small, compact design to cope with the curve of the shade.

2 Pour a little paint onto a sheet of glass or a plate and use a roller or small sponge to coat the stamp evenly. Use special stamping paint, suitable for use on fabrics. Practice using the stamp on a piece of spare fabric or ideally on an old lampshade that you no longer want.

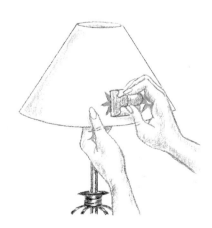

3 Hold the lampshade in such a way that it doesn't bend under the pressure of the stamp, and gently but firmly press the stamp onto it. Repeat around the shade, always re-coating the stamp with paint before applying it to the shade. Work away from the stamp you have just made so that you don't smudge the paint.

Variation: Stenciling a shade

- Again, choose or make a stencil that suits the curve and size of the lampshade. Using fabric or stencil paint and a stencil brush, hold the stencil firmly against the shade and stipple in the paint.
  Practice on something first to find the best way of achieving the effect you want. Repeat the design around the shade, working away from the image you have just stenciled so you do not smudge the paint.

Project 24

Painted floors

Varnished floorboards are attractive, but a painted floor can be a real showpiece. The art is not in the painting, but in the planning and preparation ...

You will need:
- Eggshell paint
- Mineral spirits
- Cloth
- Low-tack masking tape
- Yardstick for marking the pattern
- Pencil and eraser
- Large paint brush
- Non-yellowing oil-based varnish

1 Prepare the wood for painting. If the floor is bare new wood, seal any knots with knotting solution, sand lightly, and prime with wood primer. If the floorboards are already varnished or painted, sand them down to provide a key for the new coat of paint.

2 Apply a base coat of eggshell paint in the lightest shade of the colors to be used (in this case, minty cream). Paint the entire area. Leave it to dry overnight.

3 Plan your design to scale on graph paper and then measure and mark the design in pencil on the floor.

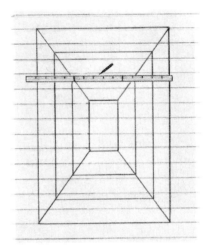

4 Using low-tack masking tape, outline the areas of the design where the second color (in this case,

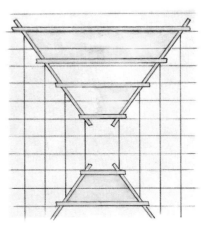

pale green) is to be applied and then paint in these sections. Leave it to dry before removing the masking tape. If two coats are needed to achieve a strong opaque color, leave the first coat to dry overnight. If any runs have crept under the tape, they can be wiped off at this stage with a cloth dabbed in mineral spirits.

5 Mask off the areas of the design where the third color (in this case, the darker green) is to be applied and then paint in these sections. Leave to dry before removing the masking tape.

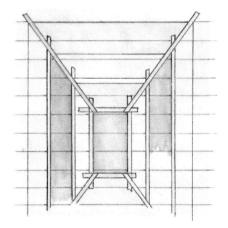

6 For extra protection (especially for light colors) apply two or more coats of a non-yellowing oil-based varnish. Dead-flat varnish has been used here.

Project 25
Shelving

Even if you lack the confidence to knock a nail into the wall, you can create useful and stylish shelving. Why restrict yourself to boring brackets when, with a little imagination, you can build shelves from almost anything sturdy enough to bear some weight?

Here storage jars, small chests of drawers, and wine racks all take the strain — making your shelves work doubly hard for you by offering extra storage space into the bargain.

Right: Perfect for the home office, these basic chests of drawers were given a quick wash of color and then put to use storing staples and other small items.

Left: Glass storage jars can be filled with anything from pebbles or colored stones to brightly wrapped candy (if you think you can resist them) to create quirky, decorative shelving supports.

Above: Simple wine racks make perfect shelving supports for the dining room or kitchen, and, luckily, they look as effective empty as they do when they're full!

Index